20 TIPS
FOR CORPORATE CHICKS

Angela Pierce

Illustration by Michael Chapoton

∞ INFINITY
PUBLISHING

ISBN 978-0-7414-7407-0 Paperback
ISBN 978-0-7414-7408-7 eBook

`Printed in the United States of America   .

Published April 2012

INFINITY PUBLISHING
1094 New DeHaven Street, Suite 100
West Conshohocken, PA 19428-2713
Toll-free (877) BUY BOOK
Local Phone (610) 941-9999
Fax (610) 941-9959
Info@buybooksontheweb.com
www.buybooksontheweb.com

Thank you for loving me while I have grown into the woman I am

I love you Blaine, Amelie, and little peanut

Special thanks to my parents, sisters, & friends for their support
in all my hair brained endeavors

Can't forget Scott Semegran, who helped me through
the crazy publishing maze

Tips

If you are like most women, you're in constant struggle with how to manage your life, your career, and the world's expectations of you. Add to this struggle the desire to be the best in every area of your life, and you often have a mess of a mental state, occasional breakdowns, and constant questions about what you can do to advance your career without giving up on everything else.

The truth is, most of us—and our male counterparts, too—have to sacrifice *something* if we want to be successful in corporate America. However, there are some hints and shortcuts we can learn from women who have found successful strategies as their careers progressed. I personally have learned much watching women in business, especially those whom I have admired. I have been fortunate in my own career to have been surrounded by a strong network of people who gave me countless opportunities to succeed. I was promoted to Vice President of a billion dollar company before the age of thirty and was the Chief Financial Officer for another company at the age of thirty six. I have an MBA, a CPA, and I have made both smart moves and a fair number of mistakes in my career. This book takes the nearly twenty years' worth of pitfalls and successes I've experienced and compiles a list of simple tips to help you succeed as you navigate through the ranks of corporate America..

Not every tip is for everyone, as we are all different and have already reached varying levels in our career. Some tips may even strike you as "off the mark," but I believe that every woman has the ability to reach great heights in their career and each woman will do so in a different way. So the tip that may seem unhelpful or even wrong to you might be exactly what the next woman needs to advance her career. So keep an open mind and I hope you will have at least one "Ah ha!" moment while reading through the next twenty tips.

Tip 1: Speak Up

What does that mean?

Women need to speak up in business. And while I am as altruistic as the next feminist, it doesn't mean for women's rights. Women simply need to open their mouths and share their ideas and opinions. Women spend countless hours in countless meetings listening to countless men go on and on about so many topics and issues in which they aren't even expert. The expert is often sitting right next to them, but she never says a word. Now, don't get me wrong, there are many great men managers and most of my mentors are men. We shouldn't have any issues with men sharing their opinions. In fact, most women could learn by watching them. But this is a book for women, so let's get to it. Why don't women share their ideas? Here are a few theories:

- I'm afraid I'll be wrong or I won't have the right information.
- The other team members seem more confident; they should speak.
- I'll just discuss my ideas with specific individuals later in private.
- I don't want to cause any waves or conflicts.
- My ideas won't add any value; everyone already knows the points I would make.
- Basically, I'm scared to speak in front of a group.

There may be others, but let's try to address these fears now and maybe hint at other concerns in the process. We'll start with the first fear: "I'm afraid I'll be wrong or I won't have the right information." Now, I'm not going to lie to you, occasionally you *will* be wrong. We are all wrong sometimes. But if we didn't try to participate, make decisions, or ask questions for the fear of being wrong, this country wouldn't be what it is today. The key to addressing this concern is to be decisive in your level of participation during the discussion.

If you fear you don't have the right information, ask questions. Questions are a very effective means of communication during a group discussion. There may even be others in the group making incorrect assumptions which could be cleared with your question, thereby fueling a larger discussion. So don't be afraid to ask, in the event you feel you have inadequate information. If you have time prior to the group discussion, do your homework. Make sure you understand the process or issue to be discussed and perform your own analysis or assessment of the issue. The more educated you are on the issue, the more value you can add to the discussion, and ultimately the organization. For example; say you are attending a meeting to discuss the marketing materials for a new advertising campaign. Prior to the meeting perhaps you should ask others about previous marketing campaigns; what worked, what didn't, how long the process took from concept to market. Perhaps you could do some analytical research on the cost and return of the current campaign or a previous one. Any information you gather prior to the discussion will improve your ability to contribute.

Now as far as being wrong, I've been wrong more often than I'd care to admit. But, what I've learned during the process is that you shouldn't be afraid to say "I'm not certain, I'll have to get back with you" or "While I don't know the answer to *that*, I do know *this* and *this* and *this*, which may help in the discussion." My all-time favorite response when I was wrong would have been to say nothing. However, now I realize that if you never make a mistake, you're simply not making enough decisions. (Of course, a caveat should ideally be "well-informed and educated decisions.") Write this piece of advice on a post-it note, stick it to your wall, and look at it every time you're afraid.

On to fear number two: "The other team members seem more confident; they should speak":

Confidence is something we could all use, no matter our job description or level in our organization. However, confidence does not mean accuracy. While we all know this to be true, it is difficult to say anything which may be in conflict with another person's comments when those comments are shared with greater confidence.

There are two strategies here: one, work on your own confidence level; and two, learn to contribute in a forum where others in the group have greater confidence than you. Remember, your ideas may be spectacular, but until you are comfortable communicating, no one will hear them.

There are two effective ways to increase your confidence: through external power and internal power. External power is where you focus on the external world's view of you. Now sure, your mother told you it doesn't matter what others think, but that's not always true in business success. Assess why you believe others might not see you the way you'd like to be seen and focus on that area. If you believe others will instead be comfortable with your approach, it will increase your confidence in open communication. This is where Toastmasters, professional coaches, and simple practice in front of the mirror can help.

The second strategy is by ramping up your internal power. This is where you gain confidence by focusing on the project or a specific area of the company where you lack confidence. The more you learn, the greater your confidence. This may mean sitting down with an expert in the organization and taking a crash course in processing or technical aspects. If it's a broader issue, you may be able to take a formal class. Either way, the key to gaining internal power is through knowledge. The stronger your confidence, the more likely you are to spread great ideas into the organization.

Next let's look at "I'll just discuss my ideas with specific individuals later in private":

Occasionally, this is the correct approach, especially if you believe your ideas may be perceived as negative by someone in the room, or if they involve confidential information. However, if your strategy to speak with a person one-on-one later is fear motivated, you need to stop that train and share your ideas. Part of your responsibility as a team member is to brainstorm, share ideas, and support the organization in reaching the best conclusion. If you're holding back ideas or input that may be valuable to finding the right solution for the company, you're not only limiting your success in the organization but you're limiting the company's success as well. Now not every bit of input you provide will be groundbreaking, but if one of your ideas helps fuel a greater outcome, it will have been worth the effort.

"I don't want to cause any waves or conflicts":

Now no one likes conflict, well almost no one. However, it is perfectly reasonable to disagree with the status quo when you feel that the status quo is harmful or inaccurate. In fact, most great moves forward in history were realized while questioning current methods. A very effective way to broach a controversial topic or suggestion is through a technique called the "auditor approach." Ask the group, team, or coworker why the process or topic at hand is the way it is. It is important that the "why" be asked in an innocent, nonjudgmental manner. Continue to ask as many "why" questions in an effort to lead the other party towards your idea or suggestion. When you finally make a comment or suggestion, you may even pose it as a question. Your objective is to gain the other party's support or, at a minimum, their willingness to consider your idea or comment.

If you are dealing with a classic hothead, good luck to you! Since hotheads and egotism go together, remember that, as with a nervous dog, the best way to calm an ego is to stroke it.

Consequently, your best chance to win support for a controversial or conflicting idea from a hothead is to ask them to partner with you in your approach. If you are able to convince them of the positive impact their expertise or support would have on the approach, you may gain their support. Speaking from personal experience, going head-to-head with a hotter head than yours is a recipe for a bad head ache and a very stressful day. So try the collaborative approach first, and if unsuccessful, choose your battles wisely.

Next up: "My ideas won't add any value; everyone already knows the points I would make."

Never ever, ever, *ever* assume your ideas won't add value. Everyone has his or her own perspective and comes at an issue with different experiences, education, assumptions, and expectations. Your idea may not be the one that drives the company forward and you may even get an occasional snicker. However, collaboration and brainstorming are some of the most important processes in problem resolution and wouldn't occur without everyone's participation. If you want to be part of the solution or contribute in a larger way, you must offer your thoughts and ideas.

That being said, do not go on and on with a point or idea once it has been offered to the group. Likewise, do not continue to push an agenda on others that has already been considered and dismissed. A good rule of thumb is three times: do not bring up a point or suggestion more than three times with the same group. Just keep a count in your head and bite your tongue when you want to bring it up a fourth time. Instead, turn your focus to the other discussions at hand and support your team in the brainstorming process.

"Basically, I'm scared to speak in front of a group":

You won't *always* need to speak in front of a group. When possible, funnel your ideas through a trusted source such as a colleague or your supervisor. Remember, you don't have to be the loudest voice in the room to be part of something great. However, if you have a deep-seated fear of speaking in front of a group, you should practice and capitalize on opportunities to conquer your demons and hone your skills. Giving a short, well prepared and rehearsed presentation on a topic you are intimately familiar with is a good way to start.

You may even want to schedule a formal discussion with a peer or your boss and walk them through a formal presentation on one of these issues you are trying to address. A scheduled meeting might add an additional level of anxiety, but will eventually assist you in becoming more comfortable with these types of events. And always come with a presentation or talking notes if you believe you may be in an uncomfortable position. This will ensure you stay on track and cover all of the relevant points, versus falling to your nerves and missing a good portion of your objective. There is nothing more frustrating than leaving a meeting and thinking "I should have said this and I should have said that..." A formal set of notes will mitigate the risk of this outcome.

I know it is easy enough to *tell* someone else to speak up and put their neck on the line, but much harder to actually go do it. So here are a few more tips to ensure you are successful.

- Wear a string on your finger, or something symbolic as a physical reminder to speak up. Next time you are sitting in a meeting, fixate on that object until you finally share your thoughts. (My personal reminder is a $10.00 painted ring purchased at a retail store which carried accessories far too cool and young for my age. Find your own string.)
- Simply open your mouth and utter one single word or syllable. Everyone will turn and look at you; that's the bad part. The good part is you will probably finish your

sentence and your idea may be a wonderful contribution to the discussion.

So share your voice and don't be afraid to communicate your ideas and opinions. If after this discussion and some practice you're still nervous, then perhaps you need to focus even more on your confidence. And if confidence is your goal, the next tip is for you.

Tip 2: Expand Your Mind

What does *that* mean?

People say knowledge is power, and man, is that true. However, it's not the knowledge which creates the power; it's the confidence from having knowledge that does the trick.

Knowledge is king, knowledge is truth, and one should know thy self. All the great philosophers are in agreement on the virtues of knowledge. For our purposes, let's focus on you and how knowledge might assist in career advancement.

To expand your mind means to really learn something new. While a more creative person would say there are endless ways to expand your mind, I am an accountant by nature, so let's boil it down to three general strategies for gaining knowledge.

1) Learn, hone, and expand your technical skills
2) Develop your personal life
3) Go through an education process

First, learn, hone, and expand your technical skills. This is the easiest to grasp of the three strategies and is certainly the most direct route to confidence and career advancement. You should always be looking for ways to improve your technical skills. And "technical" doesn't mean you need to work on your rocket science or quantum mechanics skills. A technical skill is simply something that can be used in your current or maybe a future job that will make you more efficient, will allow you to solve problems in a more creative way, or will allow you to more effectively communicate with peers.

I'll give you an example. During the mid 1990s I was an internal audit manager and during my first assignment in a new company (and, for that matter every audit assignment in that company thereafter), I was completely overwhelmed with massive amounts of data. The data was inconsistent in format and incomplete across multiple systems. Processes were completely manual, everything was on paper, and we were sitting on a gigantic pile of literally thousands of records to both audit and build processes around. Microsoft Excel was helpful, but that software tool simply was not robust enough to help with our data plight. So I decided to learn Microsoft Access. I figured it couldn't be too difficult since it came with Microsoft Office, and I wasn't a complete dummy, so I took an online tutorial and went to work. Needless to say, the tool was a huge help in developing a database to track and monitor progress as well as in creating a process to perform audits. The first year we created the processes (which were still largely used eight years later), and our team generated over $9 million dollars in incremental cash as a result of the audits we performed. I still use Microsoft Access today and amaze coworkers with my technical skills.

Now your new or enhanced knowledge doesn't need to be technical, but it should in the end provide you with a concrete skill which can improve your future performance, or at the very least increase your confidence. So your technical skill could simply be that you become more accomplished in the acronyms used in your industry, or you begin reading trade magazines, or any other thousands of efforts which may allow you to become a greater expert in whatever it is you are doing or want to do in the future.

The second idea is develop your personal life. No one is more fun to work with than someone who is happy with their personal life. Think about the times in your life when things were really good outside of the office. You were probably more focused at work and more positive in your approach to problems, both of which increase your chances of success. That's not to say you have to have the perfect relationship, 2.5 kids (or no kids, if that's your dream), and be in perfect physical shape, but small changes can have a big impact on your performance. If you're not sure what sort of personal development is right for you, here are some ideas;

- Take a class you've always wanted to take: French, painting, sailing, etc.
- Join a social club: book club, sewing club, outdoors group, etc.
- Work on your romantic life: go on dates with your partner or online dating
- Work on your physical life: work out, change your eating habits, stop smoking
- Get a pet
- Write a book
- Just get out and do something new!

Joining Toastmasters or a professional networking group is not the same thing as developing your personal life, however. These types of activities are primarily for businesses, not your personal life, so don't fool yourself. I know, I know: it's hard to believe you even have *time* for a personal life. Believe me, I didn't have one either for a large part of my career, but you need one if you're going to stay sane enough to be valuable to your employer.

Additionally, your confidence and attitude in business will begin to wane if you have no personal life. You will blame it on the job, company, or your boss, while all the while you are the only one who can really do anything about it.

The opportunities which always worked best for me were ones which required a small commitment but a regimented meeting time, such as violin lessons for one hour per week. Any real music commitment would have required practice in addition to a one hour class, which I never did, and probably some talent, which I didn't have. Who was I kidding; I'm an accountant and never got past "Turkey in the Straw" on the violin. But that didn't matter, because I had fun and enjoyed myself doing something completely not work-related. Or, when you can't find any time in the week, adopt a hobby to pursue in the evening at home, such as sewing or baking. As a matter of fact, it is precisely 10:52 p.m. right now as I write this line. The baby is asleep and I have a 9:00 a.m. meeting, but this is my personal time and I am writing a book that hopefully will help some other poor overworked soul find her place in life as well.

Third option: you can go through an education process. This is by far the most direct route to gaining knowledge, confidence, power, and a host of other great executive attributes. However, it is the largest commitment, too, and before embarking on any education process you should be fully committed, because failure in completing a process will be difficult emotionally as well as possibly financially.

The most typical education processes are formal education, advanced degrees, internships, and certifications. These processes differ from simply taking a class because a large part of the confidence and power you gain isn't from the technical skills learned, but from the sweat and tears earned during the entire process. You should expect a process to be stressful, difficult, and time consuming. However, when you complete it, you should feel like a million bucks and your confidence and knowledge will greatly benefit from your endeavors. Make sure you have thoroughly considered the time and energy that will be required before embarking. It is also important to gain support from your friends and loved ones before starting an intensive education process, or else you may crack like an egg under the pressure.

Now, when you're done with the great mind-expansion, let's talk about another tip that might help you move up in the organization.

Tip 3: Quack Like a Duck

That's right.

Put your hands under your armpits and walk through the halls squawking like a giant duck, certain to get their attention. Of course that's a joke, but also a great visual. In order to gain the position you really want, you need to perform as though you are already in that position. Thus if you have feathers and voice a loud quack, they will eventually have no choice but to call you a duck. Remember, people don't promote you to a job, they promote you to the job you're already doing.

You've probably heard the old saying, dress for the job you want. Well, your dress, while having some impact, isn't the trait that will gain you the promotion. You need to act like a manager if you want the manager position and lead like a vice president if that's your goal. There are a few notable challenges when voicing your newly found quack. The most prominent challenge is how to not overstep your grounds and possibly offend another employee—or worse, your boss—by acting as though you've already gained the promotion. The second, more personal question is how do you muster the confidence, and what do you really need to do to nurture your inner quack?

As for the first problem, how do you not step on another's toes? This is not always easy. There are two types of bosses: the one that will give you the opportunity to grow, speak highly of you, and will help you in your career; and then there is the other type of boss, the one that houses insecurity, takes credit for your work, and will rarely help you in your career advancement.

Now, if your boss, though difficult to work for, is respected by the rest of the organization, then you too must be careful to support him or her for both of your sakes. The best strategy you can implore in this instance is to support others while helping your boss's cause. If your boss is well respected by others, then they have probably earned it through hard work of their own or, at a minimum, sharing their employees' work, which they were wise enough to realize would benefit the organization. Either way, it is important not to overstep a well respected boss's bounds, because higher-ups may perceive you as "land grabbing", disrespectful, a "know it all", or worse, some sort of competition.

With a well respected boss, you could develop the process or analysis that you believe reflects the abilities of the position you want, and share it with your boss at a level which would require your support for any secondary analysis. For example, I was a Senior Manager of Revenue Accounting and had a wonderful boss, who I wasn't sure was really supportive of a promotion for me, maybe because he thought backfilling my current role would be a massive headache. So, I started to produce executive level presentations and summaries—which I believed were pretty representative of what a Director level person would develop—on a monthly basis for our department. Of course, these were shared with my boss, and lo and behold he began to distribute the data as well. If there were any detailed questions about the information, our department became the visible source for the data. I was promoted to Director the next year, though I was quacking like a Director long before the promotion.

If your boss is not supportive of your growth and is not well respected by the organization, I am so, so sorry for you. However, there is still hope. The difference between this scenario and the one in which your boss is respected is that in the uglier scenario you may have to spread your wings without your boss. For example, when an opportunity arises, send a copy of the analysis you recently completed to your boss simultaneously with the other person or organization the analysis is intended to benefit. In the communication perhaps you can say, "My boss wanted to ensure you had this data as quickly as possible since you are meeting with the customer tomorrow; let us know if you have any questions." Perhaps, you could also mention completion of the analysis in the hall to a member of the other organization and let them know you'll get it to them as soon as you've had a chance to review it with your boss. The important points are: ensure your boss is completely in the loop, as they must gain credit for requesting the analysis; the efforts must be wholly in the spirit of helping the company; and the other organization or person should know you're intimately involved in the analysis, process development, or whatever other great accomplishment you want to communicate. Your efforts must appear and actually be for the benefit of the organization (no one likes a "know-it-all" or "self-glorifier"). By taking this approach, you ensure your message is delivered without any negative associations which could be present with a less-than-respected boss, and you have continued to maintain the lines of authority by keeping your boss in the loop.

No guarantees this will work. You may still have issues with a very insecure boss in this scenario. They may feel you've tried to go around them or operate without their approval. This part is up to you. You must assess how sensitive your boss may be and adjust accordingly. For example, you may need to ensure your boss gains credit for the work or the idea in a large way. That's fine; everyone wants to be part of the solution in a big way. Your goal here is simply to ensure you are part of that solution as well.

If the next step in your career requires a larger project, management of a process, or problem resolution, the same tactics are applicable. You will need to include your boss in the idea and process in whatever way possible to ensure he/she is supportive of the process, even if he/she doesn't feel altogether supportive of your growth.

If the position you're aiming for is really a leadership position in the company, then don't forget a few additional tips:

- Everyone wants to be part of something great
- People appreciate others who are willing to take a chance
- Others respect those who can admit when they've made a mistake
- Everyone wants a voice in the process

If you can remember these concepts, the people around you will usually be on board with your quest for leadership greatness.

One last reminder: no one likes a person who keeps complaining about how he or she should hold a higher role in the company, and that means *nobody*. If you are quacking like a duck and still not getting the promotion, it is very possible that you are being perceived as not ready because you continually verbalize that you deserve something and are being held back. Remember, your supervisor needs to want to promote you and no one wants to deal with a person that is constantly asking for a promotion. Let me tell you first hand as a manager for many years, the best time to discuss the opportunities for promotion are during your review or during a one-on-one meeting with your boss. While you may proactively schedule the meeting to discuss career growth with your boss, which is an excellent idea, you shouldn't push for more than two discussions per year regarding this topic. Remember, there may be other considerations you aren't privy to.

And just when you finally receive that promotion and you're on cloud nine, allow me to bring you back down to earth and provide the next tip.

Tip 4: You Are a Pawn

You heard right: you are an expendable foot soldier.

I always say my boss would replace me in a minute and hire a monkey to do my job if he thought the monkey would do the job just as well for a few dollars less. Now, I usually bathe more often than a monkey and get along well with my boss, but the point is the same: at the end of the day, everyone in a company is simply a tool for a particular set of purposes and *everyone* can be replaced.

In a game of chess, (which by the way, I am terrible at, so I shouldn't really be making these sorts of analogies) you rely on your pawn to hold a position, protect important assets, and move the team forward. But, if you lose one pawn you just say "Shoot!" and simply look to another pawn to pick up the slack. It's the same in corporate America. Now, good leaders really do appreciate their employees and a strong leader knows when they have a star employee in the group, but the first priority as a manager is to the company and second to the employees. On the flip side, a great company can only exist with great employees. To expand even further, there are two sides to this discussion.

As a manager, your first priority is the company's health and wellbeing. This means if a great employee quits, you will look to replace them with another great employee. If you are one of those people who believe the company couldn't live without you and would fall apart if you were to leave, let me hand you a small dose of reality: everyone is replaceable in sixty days. Maybe a few balls will drop, sure. However, eventually the balls will be picked up and the new person doing your job might have innovative ideas and improve on what you've left behind. You can validate this yourself by remembering the last time you took over a new role.

You probably thought at some point, "Boy, we sure have made improvements since I've taken over this role." It's very possible that the person who held the role prior to your arrival believed they were irreplaceable. In a well run company, each new person who takes on a new role should improve it from its current state. That doesn't mean the previous employee wasn't wonderful, but for the management team, it is first and foremost about the business. If it were all personal it wouldn't be called "Corporate America," it would be called "People America."

As an employee, your first priority is to yourself and your family (or maybe your dog, or free time, or whatever else gets you up in the morning). And never forget that you are a pawn. Though it may be difficult to stomach, your company would lay you off if it made the right business sense, whatever that might mean for your company. For example, I've actually made a decision in my career to not lay an employee off because he was so central to the culture of the company that I felt it would damage morale more than benefit the bottom line. In this instance, the decision to keep the employee was based largely on his personality, but the benefit to the company was a business decision. Likewise, your allegiance should always be first to yourself. You may love the people you work with and you may love your job, but that does not mean your absolute dying allegiance should be to your company. It's important to remember this when you are being asked to perform duties in your current position which make you uncomfortable or require a greater personal sacrifice than you may be willing to give. If you ever doubt this, think of those auto workers who dedicated more than thirty years of their lives to one company and were given the boot one day for the health of the business. That's not bashing the auto makers; it's what they had to do for the health of the company. But certainly many of those employees felt betrayed and didn't guess that they were pawns.

Now with all this hoopla about being a pawn, don't take away a cynical feeling from this tip. Ideally, you'll love both your job and everyone you work with. If you are able to find happiness in your career, then you have accomplished a great feat. Just keep your third eye open at all times and don't allow your commitment to the company to overshadow your commitment to yourself.

I was recently in a stressful position in my company and the stress was funneling down in a large way to my staff. One of my stronger employees came in and said, "I'm tired of being a pawn in this game; it's just too hard right now." I gave her this next tip.

Tip 5: Chaos Creates Opportunity

How so?

Well, the more insane the environment you are currently working within, the greater the opportunity for success, be that promotions, bonuses, or whatever else. In two different instances during my career when I received relatively large financial bonuses, the companies were going through a large transition, the work was difficult, and there was a tremendous amount of uncertainty to the position.

Spending an entire career in finance and seeing the various incentive plans and promotions offered across organizations, I've noticed it is definitively true that companies pay the biggest bonuses and provide the greatest growth opportunities when they have to. When times are good, people earn good bonuses and annual merit increases are present, but the really big opportunities come when the company is under duress. That is to say, companies provide these opportunities when the going is tough and they are in jeopardy of losing their employee talent. Remember, you are a pawn for a particular purpose and there are times when that purpose is vital to the company's survival or success.

This isn't to say that just because chaos suddenly engulfs the organization that you can walk into your boss's office and demand a raise, but the greater the chaos, the more important employee stability becomes to the organization.

As mentioned above, I've been fortunate financially on two occasions in my career. In the first, I worked at a bank which was closing its office effective December 31st of a certain year (no need to give away my age here). We were told about the office closing in August. I was living far from my family, was living pay check to pay check, and looking for a new job back home in Texas at the time. Now the bank had a number of customers to serve and had to transition accounts to other offices prior to the year's end. So, as incentive to maintain its key employees during this period, the bank offered me a $10,000 bonus to stay with the company through December 31st. For a person who couldn't pay their most recent $35 American Express bill, that bonus may have well been a million dollars. There was no way I would leave before that bonus was earned. I planned well and started my new job on January 3rd, two thousand miles from my old job. What a whirlwind winter, full of both chaos and opportunity.

In the second opportunity, the company was being acquired by another company and I was on the team which was tasked with ensuring the acquisition was completed without issue. My position would certainly be eliminated as part of the acquisition, so I was essentially being asked to work myself out of a job. Consequently, the company offered a bonus, which would be earned if I were laid off by the company as a result of the acquisition. The bonus was pretty large compared to my salary at the time. I had the summer off that year, and boy would I go through that sort of chaos again if it let me sleep until 9 a.m. for three months straight.

One last real world example: I have a friend who has a friend who has experienced the epitome of chaotic career movements and is still to this day benefiting from the chaos. She is an accountant, and her first job out of school was with Arthur Anderson, one of the largest public accounting firms, who was bankrupted for the mistakes of a few. This is one of the great business blunders in America history. With over eighty years in business and 85,000 employees worldwide, one scandal took down the entire organization and changed the accounting field overnight. (By the way, all of the changes to the industry have simply led to higher costs for firms and no greater controls than before.) The accountant left Arthur Anderson earlier in her career to work for a little company called Enron. Bless her heart; she was young, probably naïve, and nowhere near the scandals when they occurred. Nonetheless, the two companies on her resume are Arthur Anderson and Enron. Last I heard she was on the "lights out" team at Enron, ensuring assets were disposed of and any value realized. My guess is she received more stay bonuses than anyone you've ever met. An extreme example, but you get the idea.

The lesson here isn't to put up with any level of chaos and uncertainly in your organization at the chance of a payoff or promotion, because it doesn't always happen. However, you should look for signs during chaotic times to assess the potential for opportunities prior to making any rash decisions about your current position. A few of the signs that an opportunity might present itself are:

- The company is considering going public
- The company is talking with other companies in the industry and you believe it could lead to some sort of combination of the two companies
- There has been a mass exodus of employees who either do your particular job or your group has been reduced to a few key individuals for whatever reason
- A large partnership of some sort has been created with another company in which your skill-set is necessary to the process
- The company has recently undergone a large scale restructuring, such as bankruptcy or a change in executive management

In each of these instances it is important you believe your position is still valuable or you believe your skill-set is well respected within the organization, so that you could fill many roles in the company. No matter what, the key here is to trust your gut. It's not scientific advice, but if something smells, leave. By the same token, if you feel like you may be the last one holding down the fort, for goodness sakes, stick around to find out what might happen.

After you've assessed the unbearable level of chaos in your organization and have decided there is no foreseeable opportunity, you may decide to leave the company. In which case, this next tip is for you.

Tip 6: Don't Run from Something, Run *to* Something.

This is a very difficult tip to swallow. When you are in a horrible place in your career or company, there is no more painful advice than for someone to say "Don't take that next job!" However, this is the advice you might need to consider the next time you are given a new career opportunity.

At the end of the day, we are all animals and our natural first instinct during a crisis is to flee. In corporate America that normally means when the going gets rough, start looking for a new job. I am completely in support of this strategy. Your sanity and happiness is paramount, and if that means a new job, boss, or company then so be it. However, the only thing worse than a job you are completely unhappy with is a new job where you have little knowledge, have less seniority and can't stand it either.

On a personal note, I was working as a Senior Director at a time during my career when the company I was with was in some level of turmoil. I was also far overdue for a promotion to Vice President. I had a few peers who had recently been promoted in another organization to Vice President and felt certain I had contributed consistently at a minimum the same level they had. I only provide this background because it is a very typical situation in which an employee might be driven to look outside their current employer. As you might have expected, I began a massive search, far and wide, for anything that had the title "Vice President" in it. I was living in Austin, Texas at the time (a great city, I might add). I found an opportunity as Vice President for a tax firm in Dallas, Texas (not as great a city, I might add). Now, tax is a very boring field. I suspect even if (or perhaps especially if) you are not a finance person by trade, you'll believe me when I say, *very* boring. However, it was a Vice President opportunity and it paid a little more, though not enough to really upgrade my wardrobe. It was a tough decision, but in the end I turned the opportunity down. A friend gave me the tip that I am giving to you now, and she was right. I had a one-on-one discussion with my boss at the time and shortly thereafter was promoted to Vice President.

So the moral of this story is you should never take a new career opportunity simply because you are unhappy in your current position. You should instead be excited and inspired by the idea of your next role. You're taking the right next step if your gut instinct is to run to the next role. Your consistent thought should be "I can't wait to get in there and try something new" versus "I can't wait to get out of the trap I'm currently in."

Now, there are exceptions to this rule, obviously:

- If you are afraid of losing your current position due to downsizing
- If you must take the next role due to a required move or personal situation
- If you are in an uncomfortable or abusive career situation
- If you go home every night and cry yourself to sleep due to the misery of your current role

Basically, do not fall into the trap of convincing yourself that this next role is a really great opportunity, when you suspect in your deepest heart you are simply settling.

In the example earlier, my friend imparted these words of wisdom upon me. Later in her career she ignored her own advice and ran from a position. She was working at a manufacturing company as a Corporate Controller. The office was an hour and a half commute from her home each way, the environment was strenuous, and the management very lackluster. She left the company to work for a startup organization in which there were some stock options but a fairly sizeable level of job insecurity. When she took the position she seemed excited, enough. Looking back, there was a fair amount of self convincing in her voice as she described the new opportunity. She had more recently indicated a desire to find stability and start planning more aggressively for retirement. So this new job seemed a *little* counterintuitive, but it was closer to her home and there was upside in the stock options, so who was I to question her motives. Not long after, the risk of job loss due to economic conditions drove her to leave this position to work for a quasi government financial institution. She described the opportunity for promotion within her new company as requiring a death of old age within the organization, but she eventually gained some stability, which she had been wanting for years. There is nothing worse than a rebound job (well, maybe a rebound boyfriend), so run to your next opportunity, no looking back.

Tip 7: You Are Not Their Den Mother

As much as you would like to protect your employees from the evils of the world and the monsters in the closet, you are not their den mother. You are their boss. If you don't have employees reporting directly to you just yet, we'll work on moving you into management in other tips. This one is specifically reserved for when you are managing your own staff.

As women we are raised to be empathetic, supportive, and nurturing. After watching my two-year-old daughter build relationships with her baby dolls, I began to believe these traits are truly innate, though admittedly stronger in some women than others. These traits, while necessary for world peace and the advancement of civilization, can sometimes weaken your ability to manage a team.

The most overt example of this risk is when managing an employee whom you feel is performing below par, but who you are unable to properly discipline for fear of causing them undue personal strain. You need to remember that as a manager, you are first and foremost a steward of the company and its goals. Once you allow your personal feelings for an employee or your "den mother instincts" for an employee to outweigh the company's objectives, you have become too emotionally attached to your employee.

So what are some things you can do to avoid becoming their den mother, you ask?

1) When an employee begins to discuss painful personal issues with you it is important to show you care about their wellbeing, as you probably already do. However, you should show this by simply being a patient listener and

when appropriate offer them personal time to deal with the situation, or whatever other work-related concessions might be appropriate given the circumstances. Do not under any condition provide them with personal advice on how to deal with the situation or offer to be a shoulder to cry on. Avoid becoming involved in their personal life and a confidant in the drama, if there is any. This is the realm for friends, sisters, and mothers, not bosses. It is not easy to hold your tongue, but remember: your job is to support the company's goals while providing a safe and productive environment for your employees.

2) Limit your interaction with employees outside of the workplace. There are a number of benefits to limiting your interaction with employees outside of the office. The most obvious is to ensure there is no appearance of favoritism or inappropriate relationship with your employee. The second is to ensure you limit bonds with your employee that may later hinder your ability to properly manage the employee or the group. Lastly, the employee may begin to see you first as a friend and secondarily as a boss. This could be disastrous. Some people ask for an inordinate amount of leeway and forgiveness from their friends. The level of forgiveness that may be required as a result of poor product, lost work time, and simple insubordination could destroy not only a potential friendship but a good employee as well. General rules of thumb on employee interaction outside the workplace are:

a. It's allowed occasionally if multiple organizations and/or varying levels of management and staff are also attending the function (such as a large group happy hour)

b. Obviously, any corporate-sponsored event is totally fine

    c. A celebration for an employee, so long as other employees are invited

    d. A get-together of some sort as a celebration of the season or a group success

    e. A get-together after work or during lunch with a single or very limited employee base so long as it is occasional and in no way becomes a routine occurrence

    f. Group family events are permissible so long as they are also non-routine in nature

    g. Reasonable levels of interaction as a result of business travel with one another

3) Do not allow their personal situation to unduly influence your management decisions. It is important to be sensitive to your employees' personal needs, such as allowing them time with their family and encouraging a healthy work/life balance. However, there is a point where consideration for their personal needs can damage the morale of the overall group or negatively impact the company's performance.

I was once working for a company in which we were implementing layoffs. If you have been in corporate America for any amount of time, you are probably all-too familiar with this process. A coworker had to make a decision to lay off one of the two people in a certain department. It would have been a difficult decision for me; both were skilled but had different skill sets. My coworker made the decision to lay off the manager, partly or maybe largely because the vice president's husband had recently lost his job and they had kids. He didn't want to be the one who led the family to a no-income scenario. Now I'm not certain how influential a factor the family's situation was in the coworker's decision, but it probably shouldn't have been a factor at all. There is no way he could have known for certain the impact to the other employee; perhaps she had a mountain of personal medical bills and was on the verge of bankruptcy, who knows. The vice president ended up leaving the company six months later, without a new job lined up. At the time the vice president left, the manager, ironically, still hadn't found a full time position.

Now it's time for the difficult part of the tip. What do you do once you realize you have become a den mother-type despite my advice? You must immediately employ the three tips above in a very aggressive way. Personal communication where you are being used as a sounding board for life advice must stop, as should personal outings beyond the office. If you are uncomfortable or are asked directly why you are becoming so distant, you can take two approaches.

    a. You can sit down with the employee and explain how your relationship should work and where you believe the appropriate limits lie for communication and fraternizing.

    b. Or, you can take the lighter approach. Simply tell the employee you are making an effort to maintain a more professional and less personal relationship with your employees to ensure you maintain good working relationships and strong morale across the group and the rest of the company.

Tip 8: Be the Lady, Not the Tramp

What does that mean?

If you are a woman in corporate America, you know what that means. The workplace is for work, not for grand displays of flesh and feminine curves. It is unfortunate when a woman who might otherwise be well respected and successful becomes limited in her career because she consistently wears a tight red mini skirt, low cut shirts, and bright green stilettos. Now every office is different, and varying regions of the country allow for more casual and perhaps stylish dress. If you're not certain what's acceptable in your office, take your cue from others. Look at the three most successful and well respected women in the office and review their attire. You probably want to dress more like those women. That doesn't mean you must copy their look or purchase high priced designer clothing; it's the theme that's important. Again, every environment is different, but here are a few general guidelines.

1. Skirts should be no shorter than three quarters down your thigh. Additionally, if you bend over and reach for your toes and you can touch the underwear covering your bottom with your hand, the skirt is too short.
2. If you lift your arms to imitate squawking like a duck due to following Tip #3 and your midriff is visible, the shirt is too short.
3. If you can see more than a hint of your cleavage, or when you lean over the desk your bra is as clear as day, your shirt is cut too low.
4. I'm only five-feet-one-inch tall, so I'm all for heels. However if there is any chance the shoes could possibly be worn by a stripper during a pole dance, save the shoes for the weekend. They are not appropriate for the office.

5. If you have to lie down on the bed to zip something, whatever it is, it's too tight.

There are probably a million other rules and it really depends on your work place. If you aren't certain whether your dress is appropriate, engage the opinions of a trusted colleague. It is better to ask someone who actually works in your environment versus a friend outside the company. They will have a more relevant view on acceptable dress in the office. Do *not* ask a man, believe me, they probably won't complain about the red miniskirt, nor will they be as painfully honest, which is what you're looking for here. Do not ask your trusted source whether they believe your dress is appropriate. No one tells a woman friend that her miniskirt is a bad idea. Ask your source for three critiques of your dress, style, or personal appearance which may be hindering your career. You might be surprised by what they reveal.

On a personal note, I was once a Senior Director in a company and had an office just down the hall from the CEO as well as a number of other executives. There were many higher ups nearby to offend. One day I was walking by the CFO's executive assistant and she giggled. Of course I had to ask what was so funny. Now, much to my chagrin, this particular executive assistant was known for her candor. She told me that my—dare I say, well this is a book for women, so here goes—my nipples were poking through my shirt. Surely this has happened to many of us and it typically isn't an issue unless it is cold. Unfortunately, office buildings are notoriously freezing. Needless to say, I was completely mortified. I had always believed myself to be a well dressed professional and fairly considerate of office attire. I marched right down to the unmentionables store that evening and purchased the most restraining and uncomfortable bra I had owned in years. The moral of the story is you can't see everything that might offend, so you need to ask others for their opinion, even if you're pretty certain this tip isn't for you.

One last comment on dress: you are a woman and should be comfortable dressing, looking, and acting like one. Some women sell themselves short by dressing masculine or minimizing feminine habits, such as makeup, accessories, and general style. If you think you might be one of these women, then take heed of my next tip.

Tip 9: Don't Be Afraid to Be Feminine

No, no, this doesn't mean you have to wear three coats of mascara and pink ruffles. However, one of the benefits to being a woman in the workplace is that you're actually a woman in the workplace. Feminine attributes carry a considerable amount of influence.

Many women are completely afraid to present any semblance of femininity. But you must remember, much of corporate America is men and men are still men, even in the workplace. They won't routinely ask you to go play golf or watch the game with them, even if you come to work in a Yankees ball cap carrying a nine iron. But they will probably listen to your suggestion when proposed in a non-confrontational, feminine voice.

What exactly constitutes feminine? It's hard to say because it varies by individual. Think about the tone of voice or facial expressions you use when trying to convince your partner to agree with you. Personally, I typically implore a softer, patient, and more supportive voice. And smile—don't forget to smile. A woman's smile can often reduce the tension in any work related confrontation or heated discussion.

Of all the tips, this is probably one of the most difficult to assess because we try so hard in business to be tough and show that we can do whatever a man can do. A woman *can* do whatever a man can do, sometimes even more, and often with less destruction in the process. If you don't believe me, the next time you're speaking to a male counterpart and don't agree with his comments, try disagreeing with a smile on your face and with a softer tone than your typical office voice. A smile is difficult to find when in disagreement, so practice such discussions in your mirror at home until you find the right tone and smile that works for you. Then try it at work, and pay attention to how he responds. Because he is less likely to feel challenged and attacked, he will be more open to a discussion on the issue. It is difficult for a man to execute this tactic since the basis of testosterone seems to be challenge.

Regarding dress and personal appearance, first and foremost you should always be comfortable and confident. If that means you don't feel comfortable in heels, makeup, or a lavender silk shirt, then perhaps you could find a necklace, set of earrings, or some other feminine accent. While this comment may sound ridiculous to some of you, it can make a difference in your interactions.

Men have been admiring the female form for thousands of years. That fact hasn't changed despite all of the women's movements and fights for equality over the last few hundred years. Men enjoy being around females and often let their guard down when around a woman, more so than with men alone. The idea that men might treat you differently in this instance might be upsetting. But let's be honest, you will never be "one of the boys" no matter how androgynous your dress or how well you know your sports statistics. However, one way to continue pushing women forward in business is to leverage these seemingly negative situations. You may be more likely to get a meeting or what you want, whether it's information, agreement, or support, simply because his guard is down and you are more enjoyable to speak with than the guy in the cube next to you. I call this "Le Femme Shark Attack."

So don't be afraid to be feminine; you were born that way. However, as you'll see in the next tip, femininity can go too far.

Tip 10: Never Let Them See You Cry

Honestly, I don't know a woman in the workplace who hasn't cried at some point upon entering or after leaving the office. As a matter of fact most of the strongest women in business have cried a time or two in their career. The important thing to remember about crying is that men don't. And while even a woman boss or female coworker understands why you might cry, you should avoid crying in front of them too.

This tip is to never cry in front of your boss or other coworkers. Why? Well, men will see you as weak and even if you think they don't perceive you as weak, they will at least see you as unable to handle the stress of your current position, role, or project. Good luck getting the promotion or next opportunity if you can't handle what you have. Now, as a woman we all understand that crying has nothing to do with your ability to handle the challenge. Women cry because:

- They are angry at someone else
- They are overwhelmed
- They are tired
- They are hurt or offended
- They are experiencing hormonal changes
- They have personal things going on behind the scenes
- They are angry at themselves
- Or any other number of reasons

However, men don't respond to any of these issues above in the same way as women do and the only thing they can understand about crying is that it is an *emotional* response to something, not a rational response. Arguably it is as much a physical response as emotional, but no matter. If you're crying, then there is something going on. No matter what it is, it isn't the end of the world. This is just a job, and you need to pull yourself together.

Now, I'm sure that sound heartless to some of you, but I have cried a few times in the office and I was never proud of it. The most embarrassing time was also one of the more embarrassing points in my career. I was the Director of Finance and was in charge of the company's financial planning, budgeting, and general corporate financial operations. It was shortly after 9/11, so emotions were generally high across the country. It was about 9:00 in the morning and the CFO's administrative assistant came down to my office and said "He [the CFO] is ready for you to send the presentation for the Board meeting." To this I said "What Board meeting?" And as you would expect, she said "Uh, the 10:00 a.m. Board meeting?" I just about flipped out; I had no idea there was a Board of Directors meeting, or that I was supposed to prepare something. I made a quick call to the CFO and he gave me the rundown on what he was looking for. I ran to one of my trusted employees and explained what we needed to do: "You start putting the presentation together, I'll finish the numbers and by the way we need to be done, like, right *now!*"

We both started working and it was simply too much to do and too little time. My employee began to panic so much that she couldn't even type. I pulled her out of her chair and began banging on the keyboard. In about thirty minutes we had some semblance of a presentation and sent it to the boss as quickly as possible. About five minutes later, the Executive Assistant came down again and said "He said the numbers don't look right and you need to add this and that and that to the presentation and he needs it right away. They're sending the presentation to the Board members in just a few minutes."

OK, so some fire-drills are just too blazing to extinguish. I slowly walked to my office, shut my door, turned my back to the door (which by the way had one of those windows running the length from the ceiling to floor in it), and began to cry. About thirty seconds later I heard a knock, presumably from that pestering Executive Assistant on the glass in my window. . Now as I've told you, never let them see you cry, so I quickly picked up my phone handset and acted as though I were on the phone. After about a minute of knocking, I turned my crying face to the window, swung open the door, and yelled, "What do you want?" Of course it was the CFO, and it didn't help that he was young and pretty good looking. I just wanted to die. It only got worse when I saw a look of fear flit across his face. He reached out and gave me this stiff, sterile hug that made me cry harder. Somehow we all got through the presentation—well, all of us except my pride.

So what is the hardest part about not crying in the office? Well it's the part where the tears start streaming down your face and you have absolutely no control. So what are you suppose to do? Well, it depends on the situation.

If you are working with an employee or coworker and they begin to cry, remember you are supposed to help them grow in their professional career, and part of that task is allowing them to maintain their emotional strength in the office. When an employee begins to tear up in front of me, I very patiently tell them that everything is OK and ask them to take a break. It's good to recommend they gain their composure in privacy and that they can use an unoccupied office if that would help. Ask them to go get a cup of coffee, take a walk around the building, or anything else that may help release some of the nervous energy which has driven them to tears.

Now for yourself. If you can make it to your office or a bathroom stall to "cry it out," that often works. But as we know from my story, just because you think you have found some privacy, doesn't mean you won't have to face someone in mid-bawl. A safer strategy is to flee the building all together. If you are one of those stronger souls who are able to push the tears away, then you may not need an escape plan. See if these suggestions work:

1. The minute you feel tears begin to swell behind your eye lids or you feel your face begin to quiver, immediately take a breath and ask for a minute if you are in mid-sentence, or divert the conversation to someone else so that you may gain your composure.

2. Smile. I'm not sure how the science works, but once you bring a smile to your face it is almost impossible to not feel a little better.

3. Look slightly to the side or innocently away from the forward discussion. Do not look down; gravity isn't your friend here. Any tears near the surface will be pulled towards the ground as though they are weights hanging from your eyes.

4. Think briefly of something humorous and completely off topic. I have a standard memory from a mid 1990s sitcom episode where the main characters make a personal bet with each other. It isn't important which humorous and off topic thought you bring to your mind. You simply think of some funny event in your past for a brief moment in order to divert your attention from the cry-worthy topic at hand.

5. These events should all occur in about five seconds and may provide enough time to avoid any tears. If this doesn't work, map out your escape route and head for the door.

Whatever your strategy, remember it happens to almost every woman, but "they" don't have to know about it. And regardless of the reason for your tears and no matter how unbearable the job seems, this next tip is for you.

Tip 11: You Can Do Anything for a Year

There are three jobs on my resume where employment with the company was less than a year, it happens. However, I get more questions from hiring managers about why I left those companies in less than a year than why I decided to stay with my other companies for much longer.

No matter how difficult a job is when you first start, you can usually do anything for a year. This tip advocates that once you choose a new job, do not jump ship on the position for about a year, even though you may dislike it after a few months.

As a hiring manager, I often don't give an interview to someone who has a string or even a few jobs where they were with the company for less than a year. However, if the person looks good on paper, the reasons for which you might see merit in further discussion with the candidate would be if they left the job because:

- They didn't like the culture
- The work wasn't challenging or was boring
- The job or company changed (acquisition, lay off, change in management, etc.)
- Family driven reason (have to move, married, aging parents, etc.)
- Legal, harassment, or ethical reasons

Now regarding culture, this is an important driver to your happiness as well as your success in any position. So if the culture is a complete clash with your personality or work style, then you need to be prepared to discuss with a new hiring manager what was so difficult that it drove you to look for a new opportunity before four seasons had passed. Remember, whatever you say, the hiring manager across from you will be evaluating your answer with the knowledge of their culture, and any risk in clash will lead to your elimination as a candidate. No one wants to go through the work of hiring someone only to hire another in four months because you were uncomfortable with the company's processes or politics (or whatever other cultural phenomenon) of the company. So make sure your reason is truly cultural and not political or personal.

If the work is boring or isn't challenging, then you first need to look for additional opportunities to grow or gain responsibility within your current employer before looking elsewhere. Ask for additional duties or an interesting project. Perhaps there's an opportunity to improve the boring processes you currently manage and gain a promotion. For a hiring manager, if you tell them the job was boring, their first thought may be that you are looking for a "rock-star" job, and honestly, there aren't many of those out there. Every job has a mundane side to it. So if you are leaving because the job is boring, be sure to explain to the next hiring manager how you searched for additional opportunities or projects to provide more value to the company, but they were unavailable.

Sometimes you may feel you need to leave because the company or position's situation changes. This has likely happened to many of you in this age of companies acquiring other companies, constant change in economic conditions, and ever-shifting corporate objectives.

On a personal note, I was hired as the Vice President of Finance for a company that was planning to go public, or issuing an "IPO." I was hired to (among other things) develop their public market facing activities, such as investor relations, the investor Website, the treasury functions, etc. Just as we were about to go public, the stock markets began to severely tank and it became more evident every day that the dream was much farther away than the company had expected. I became nervous that my position might be at risk, since many of the functions I had been hired to manage weren't going to be necessary, so the first opportunity I had to make a move to a new company I took it, only eight months after being hired. Now when I describe the situation to hiring managers or recruiters, they nod their head and say "Oh yes that makes sense." Still, I am *always* asked why I left so quickly and the hiring managers tend to retain that far-away concerned look in their eye.

Be sure you know where you stand with the changes in the company or your position because the changes may not have the impact you think.

Regarding family, remember your family is your life and your job is only a job. If a family decision you've made necessitates that you leave your current employer, then that is OK. Don't ever risk family happiness for the sake of your career. Hollywood has made monumental films about the lonely and lost soul who put their careers before their families. Go see the story play out in the theatre, not in your home. I once made a decision in my career to leave a company for family reasons. I was working as a Vice President in a company when we were acquired by another, much larger company. The new CFO offered me the "opportunity of a lifetime," the Division CFO for a billion-dollar division. It was a wonderful and lucrative opportunity, which would have required extensive travel, possibly moving, and an immeasurable amount of stress. I asked the CFO if I could think about it for a few days. During those few days, I found out I was pregnant. My husband and I made the decision that the job opportunity was simply too stressful for this time in our lives. So I graciously declined and left the company. I often wonder if I made the right decision for my career, but I spend far more time with my daughter than I ever would have if I had taken the position. Now don't get me wrong, there are times to work long hours and times to sacrifice for your career, but those times should ideally be temporary. Find your balance.

Lastly, there is no reason to stay in a company where you are being asked to do something unethical or are being harassed in some way by a peer or supervisor. How you decide to resolve the issue with human resources, your boss, or through some whistle-blowing process is up to you. As with many women, I have been asked to do unethical things and have been propositioned in the workplace. After leaving a company for these reasons, you must be careful how you communicate your leaving with a new hiring manager. While we all like to believe a new hiring manager will be sympathetic, remember: they don't know you. You could be the crazy person who cries wolf, makes trouble, or is inflexible. At the very least you may be airing dirty laundry about a former employer, which is never attractive. When hiring a new employee, hiring managers tend to be risk-averse. It is important to convey that you made the decision to leave because you weren't comfortable with either the environment or the company's desire to be so aggressive in their decisions. It is less appealing to a hiring manager if in your reason for leaving you paint yourself as a victim, or as not being in control of your decision to leave.

Here are the reasons you do *not* give a hiring manager at to why you left the company after less than a year:

- The job didn't pay enough
- I didn't like my boss
- The work was too consuming

You knew how much the job paid when you took the position. So if you quit because it didn't pay enough, you are admitting to the hiring manager that you are willing to take a job you plan to leave as soon as you find a higher paying opportunity elsewhere. If this is really the reason, you need to turn the rationale into a compliment to the new opportunity, versus a slam to your prior employer. Something like "I really like my current position but I would love the opportunity to take on something even more challenging with your company [i.e. for higher pay]" is a more positive comment than "My last job was beneath me."

Disliking your boss is certainly a reason to leave a position, but never admit this. No matter how insane, unreasonable, irrational, or ignorant your boss, any hiring manager will wonder whether *you* are actually the one who is difficult to work with. Though you may have disliked your boss, he or she did rise to some level of power for some reason. So here is a tip within a tip: try to learn something from every boss you ever have. I've had fourteen bosses in my professional career, and there has only been one boss I couldn't stand, though my level of respect for each boss's abilities has varied widely, from "He's brilliant!" to "She's a great mentor!" to "What a jerk" and "He couldn't do his job without me." However, in each instance there has been an opportunity to learn something. The boss I couldn't stand was a terrible manager of his direct reports, but he managed upwards quite well. I saw him present a few times to his boss as well as the board of directors, and he was pleasant, confident, and provided a sense of competence which he may or may not have actually had. Either way, it became quite apparent in these few meetings why he was selected as President of the division.

If the work is too challenging or too personally consuming, you have the right to leave as well. However, you should not make the call on this issue until at least four to six months into the position. The first six months of a new position in a new company are full of unique challenges: simply learning your way through the chain of command, acronyms, names, who knows what, and who you can rely on for support. Until these nuances are crystallized, any position will seem overwhelming. Once you've journeyed your way through the "six-month safari," you may assess the long-term demands of the position. If the hours or work are truly too demanding, then first discuss the issue with your boss before venturing into the unknown. If you disclose the problem with work/life balance to a new hiring manager, be prepared for some scrutiny, though perhaps not directly to your face. The bottom line is that managers want someone who will be there when the work needs to be done, no matter the hours it might sometimes require. And if the work is simply too challenging and you can't see a way to overcome the daily challenges in the job or the company, this next tip is for you.

Tip 12: Be Strategic

In today's corporate environment, the word strategic is thrown around with little regard to what it really means. Surely you've heard the term used numerous times, perhaps in an executive meeting or in a description of the company. The word is typically used to describe a decision which *becomes* strategic when recommended by a member of upper management. These decisions are inevitably made in response to a challenge in the current business environment.

If you are in a larger organization, you may have entire departments with the word "strategic" in their name, such as Strategic Finance, Strategic Marketing, or the Strategic Client Team. While having the word strategic in your title is a great resume-builder, it probably doesn't describe what you do on a day-to-day basis. If you want to be more successful in business, you need to learn how and when to be truly strategic.

If you were to look the word up in Webster's you would be given this definition: "Important or essential to a plan, method, or series of maneuvers or stratagems for obtaining a specific goal or result." While this may seem very rudimentary, let's break this definition down into its subsets.

If your thinking is strategic, then your thinking is:

- Important to the plan, method, etc.
- The plan is designed to obtain a specific goal or result

Most of corporate America misses the key elements today when trying to be strategic. There often isn't a specific goal outlined, just the idea that management wants to improve the current state of business. Likewise, there is rarely a plan to reach the undefined goal. The plan is usually to be "strategic" in our thinking and decision making, which doesn't provide resolution but more often inconsistent and confused action across the organization.

In this tip we will actually walk through a detailed process plan to be strategic. This is the only step-by-step tip in the book, but when you are ready to sit down and go through a strategic planning process, hopefully this next section will help guide you.

Let's take a life like example. Amy is a Finance Manager who works in a communications service company. The company has more than 10,000 customers, who produce monthly revenues for the company of $70 million dollars. The company has monthly expenses that are directly attributable to the customers as well as expenses that are shared across all of the customers, such as administrative payroll, insurance, building expenses, and taxes.

The CEO has decided to call a management meeting to discuss opportunities to improve the company's profitability, and Amy is invited. The meeting goes something like this:

CEO: I've called you all here today to discuss the company's financial performance. It isn't where it needs to be and we need to find ways to improve our bottom line. I'd like each group to discuss opportunities in their area so that we can make some strategic decisions for the future.

Vice President of Marketing: I think if we could hire a few more project managers and if Finance approves an increase in our capital budget, we could roll out our new products more quickly and increase revenue, thus improving the company's profitability.

Vice President of Sales: I think if we increase the commission rates on our core products, our sales team's production would increase, resulting in higher revenue. The customer service for the Eastern region has been poor and I think it is causing higher customer loss. If we increase customer support staff in the Eastern region, we could better maintain the customers we currently have.

Vice President of Operations: We currently support the customer installation of so many products that I have to maintain a larger staff than I would like. If we eliminated some of the less popular products and reduced the number of new product roll-outs, we could maintain a smaller staff and reduce expenses.

CFO: We can't afford to increase staffing and capital budgets this year based on the numbers we have provided Wall Street. We will have to cut expenses in order to improve profitability quickly. I recommend we identify the lower performers within the company and reduce the overall workforce by 3% through a strategic layoff.

CEO: I want to thank each of you for your ideas. Some of these are in conflict with one another so I'd like you to get together as a team and come up with a list of strategic decisions based on what you've shared today, with the goal in mind to improve profitability this year.

Now Amy goes back to her office a little confused, knowing in the end that she will have to support the CFO and the Finance department with whatever decision is made. When the CEO said "improve profitability," did he have a certain target in mind? Is revenue growth more important or is expense reduction? What is the Finance department's role and what can that department do to help improve profitability?

If you've been in management for some time, this scenario is likely very familiar. If you've never been in a meeting similar to the one described, they are probably happening at your company and you just haven't been pulled into one yet. Remember that everyone wants the company to be successful, and everyone wants to be able to individually contribute to that success in a large and positive way. By being strategic, you can find a way to support these objectives.

How to become "strategic":

The first thing to know about being strategic is that you won't be this way all of the time. Remember, being strategic is important to the plan which is designed to obtain a specific goal or result. Some of the tasks and processes you perform on a day to day basis are more routine in nature. While even routine processes are contributing to some end goal, or they otherwise wouldn't be performed, you may feel these processes aren't contributing to the company's success in a large and positive way. Do not despair; you can still be strategic on a project-specific basis. This is an ideal strategy for those who have routine processes and deadlines and find it difficult to find creative ways to add significant value to the company.

Below is a process you can follow to help you become a more strategic thinker. You may need to alter the process to better fit your specific role in the company or your operating style. However, anyone can start with this process and develop a plan that contributes to the company's end goal in a large and positive way.

1. Find a private, quiet place in the office where you can think—an office, a vacant conference room, or an open area after hours, when few people will be on site to disrupt your process. A larger space is better than a small space. You want your ideas to be large. The space around you should mirror this objective.

2. You'll need a chair, notepad, pen, or your laptop, dry erase markers, and a whiteboard that you can sit or hang in front of you to capture ideas. It is important that this whiteboard isn't the same as the pad of paper/computer on the desk in front of you. We spend such a large part of our working life with our eyes pointing down at our desk or staring directly at a computer monitor. The objective here

is to get you thinking large and outside of your common element, so go find a whiteboard or a sufficient substitute.

3. After you have obtained your supplies and have ensured you have no pressing time deadlines, place your chair six feet from the whiteboard, sit down, take a few minutes to relax, and say to yourself, "I am going to be *strategic* today."

Now that you are prepared to open your mind and become a strategic thinker, the following steps will help guide you through the process and ensure the most creative and positive outcome. The worst thing you can do when trying to be strategic is to begin focusing on the finite and low level details of a process too early. This will inevitably limit the possible solutions and plans that could be developed to reach an end goal.

1. Ask yourself: what is the big problem here? Now this problem doesn't have to be the company's global problem. This process works for any problem where a specific goal can be developed. The problem could range from "The company's profitability is inadequate" to "My department's labor hours are too long."

2. Now, write the big problem on the whiteboard. Many would advise that your next step should be to develop a specific goal to attach to this problem, such as improve profitability by 10% or reduce labor hours by 5%. I'm actually in disagreement with this camp of thought. Instead, you first need to understand the root causes for the problem as well as the constraints surrounding the problem. This will better assist you in developing an appropriate and achievable specific goal.

3. Now, section off an area on the whiteboard and call it "Reasons."

4. Now, ask yourself why is this problem occurring and write this under the "Reasons" section.

5. Now, ask yourself why is this first "Reason" occurring and write it on the whiteboard.

6. Now, ask yourself are there possible other "Whys" for this "Reason" and write them on the whiteboard. You'll notice a pattern. This is called the "Three-question approach." Always ask yourself why something is occurring and then ask yourself why two more times. This will typically provide you with additional insight into the root cause of the problem. For each of these successive reasons it may be easiest to display them on the whiteboard in a hierarchical relationship.

7. Continue asking yourself if there are potential other reasons for the problem and write these reasons as well as their corresponding follow-up answers on the whiteboard.

Now that you've identified the reasons for this problem, you'll need to focus on developing a solution for these reasons, which in turn will assist in resolving the problem. Remember, resolving a problem requires correction of the root cause of the occurrence. This is the part of the exercise where you become strategic in your thinking.

The goal is to open your mind and think of as many potential ways to tackle these root causes as possible. Don't be concerned about whether you have the resources or expertise to carry out the corrective action plan. Remember, people throughout the company also want to contribute to the company's success, and your final recommended plan may allow others to be a part of the success. These are the questions to ask yourself about each reason. The answer to these questions could provide you with a solution to the root cause. Section off an area on the whiteboard and call it Resources. Now ask yourself the following questions:

1. What technical or system expertise do I or my department have that could be used to correct the root cause?

2. What processes am I or my department involved in that might impact or touch the root cause?
3. What information is available within the company that could be used to correct the root cause?
4. What information is not currently available that would be helpful in correcting the root cause?
5. What processes within the company may need to be changed to correct the root cause?
6. Which groups across the company might have more information about the root cause?
7. Which groups would benefit the greatest from correction of the root cause?
8. What do I know about the priorities and processes of those groups who would benefit from correction of the root cause?

As you walk through each of these questions, write any responses that come from these inquiries on the whiteboard under "Resources." The answers to these questions will not necessarily solve a problem; your objective is to open your mind and develop a plan to tackle the problem. This process is akin to brainstorming and should open you up to new ideas. If there are multiple root causes, follow the process for each issue. Oftentimes, the final solution addresses multiple root causes.

Now that you've qualified information surrounding the root cause problem, you'll use deductive problem solving to develop a plan to correct, or at a minimum address the root cause. Deductive problem solving starts with the end state in mind and works backwards by proposing a corrective action or process for each root-cause reason until you come back to the current state. By working deductively, you ensure that your final plan stays on track with the end goal of resolving the problem in mind.

Sit down in your chair, stare at the problem on the whiteboard, scan down the root cause reasons, and then scan across the resources you've identified. Take as much time as you need. You may sit there for thirty minutes or more pondering different ways in which the reasons and resources may be related.

Once you're ready, go to the whiteboard and start writing down a plan to tackle the reason or reasons, utilizing the resources you've identified as well as others that may have come to mind during your thought process. Once you're finished, sit down and create the outline for your resolution plan in a more formal manner on your notepad or computer. Once you start writing the plan down, you are moving from your strategic-thinking mode to an operational and tactical mode. The way in which you communicate and execute your plan is up to you. This tip simply suggests you be strategic in your thinking, which is important to the plan being designed to reach a specific goal or result.

In our earlier example, Amy is faced with an opportunity to be strategic after attending a management meeting. Here is an example of how this process might have unfolded in her situation.

Amy goes back to her office, closes her door, and erases the whiteboard in front of her. She outlines the following problem, reasons, and resources:

Problem: Company's profitability is too low

Reasons:

- Revenue is too low
    a. Why: New sales levels are not high enough
        i. Sales compensation doesn't drive correct behavior
        ii. Current product set isn't what customers want
            - New products can't be rolled out quickly enough

    b. Why: Customer loss/churn is too high

       i. Customer satisfaction is low in certain regions

    c. Why: Perhaps customers aren't being billed properly for current service?

       i. Company has multiple billing systems and manual processes to enter billing

- Direct customer cost is too high

    a. Why: Perhaps the company is paying vendors for services that aren't necessary?

       i. Customer can disconnect their service but the disconnection of service with our vendor is not automatic

    b. Why: Perhaps the company is paying more than it should for the services purchased from vendors?

       i. Vendor contract rates change and services may be billed to the company under old and higher rates

      ii. The company could design the customer's service in a way that the company pays a higher price than what the customer is asked to pay

Resources:

1. The Sales department has expertise in where customer satisfaction is low
2. The Sales department has expertise in the sales compensation plans
3. The Marketing, Sales, and Operations team have expertise in which products currently sell well and which products customers request, which aren't yet available
4. I have employees with strong analysis and data development skills
5. I have access to customer and unit billing details for revenue, that we use in our current processes

6. I have access to customer and unit vendor billed details for approximately half of the company's direct customer cost, used in our current processes

7. Detailed information on the second half of customer billed vendor cost is not easily available to everyone in the company

8. The Operations team would like to know the cost related to each revenue item billed so that they could design more efficient and less costly customer services

9. Sales would like to know if we aren't billing customers enough for current services

10. The Operations group would like to know when it looks like the company is being billed too much by one of its vendors

Amy sat back and pondered all that she had written on the whiteboard. It seemed evident that the Sales and Marketing team might be best equipped to come up with ideas on how to increase revenue. Amy thought her group might be able to do something with the existing revenue and cost data already collected within her group. She thought maybe her group could pull the revenue and cost data together in a way that helped the operations, sales, and accounting teams with resource items 8-10.

Amy turned to her notepad and started outlining a plan to build a process where her data and analysis team could map the individual customer revenue charges to the supporting individual customer cost charges. While this data was available for half the cost in the company, no group had the time to develop a process that combined the revenue and cost data into one file or table. It would take time and support from across the company to pull in the second half of the cost, which was not yet easily available. That would allow other groups to be part of the solution.

Once this single source of customer revenue was matched to customer cost, it would be available to every group in the company for query. Each group could look for anomalies and opportunities to bill customers where it appeared they were being under-billed and decrease cost where it looked like there were opportunities.

Amy's scenario is based on a real life example and was actually executed with the help of multiple organizations across a company over approximately four months. The combined revenue and cost data was distributed throughout the company and the result was more than $36 million dollars in added profitability during the first year.

In this example, Amy was strategic when she identified an opportunity to utilize various resources to formulate a plan to address a specific problem. However, this also required Amy to take on a project outside of her day-to-day responsibilities, which brings us to the next tip.

Tip 13: Just Do It

It seems like such a contradiction that in the corporate world of never enough, there is always more than enough work to be done. Whether you work in a large or small company, there is always more work to be completed than could be supported by the existing employee base. To be exceptionally successful, you will have to accomplish more than is expected of you. This doesn't mean just more of the same job. You will need to take on additional responsibilities. While this thought is difficult to swallow, it's much easier if you "just do it" versus finding so many excuses why extra work is not realistic.

By taking on new and additional responsibilities, you'll show your manager that you are capable of supporting multiple processes and that you are willing to grow to meet the needs of the company. In addition to showing your manager that you are more than capable of growing into a larger role, you will become a more important and valued contributor to the company's success.

If you are one of the people that already produces at a higher level than many of your peers, either through long work hours or efficient use of your time, you should be aware that everyone's expectations of you are already higher. In addition to your already over-burdensome work, personal time constraints may make it even more difficult for you to take on responsibilities beyond your current role. All that being said, for the sake of this tip, let's assume you are up to the task.

So, you should be asking yourself, *what type of new responsibility should I pursue?*

When identifying opportunities to take on new responsibility, there are at least a few criteria to consider:

1. This new responsibility should provide additional information or support to other organizations
2. You must be realistic with yourself and ensure that you have adequate manpower and expertise to take on this responsibility within your existing situation
3. This new responsibility should not be currently addressed within the organization, or, if it is being addressed, the results are incomplete and poor

It is important that this responsibility provide additional information or support to other organizations within the company. The most effective way to become more highly valued and respected is to help ease the burden or pain of other groups throughout the company. Additionally, part of your responsibility as an employee is to make your manager look good. Now, for many of you that might be difficult to stomach. Making your boss look good does not mean completing all of your work for him or her to just take direct credit. If you are successful in helping other organizations, then your boss will also be helping other organizations by allowing you to take on these new tasks. So let your boss be a hero along with you.

Taking on tasks that benefit only your department may create additional good will among your employees and close coworkers. However, these tasks limit the amount of positive exposure you might otherwise have with your manager and your manager's peers, and might require time that now can't be committed to other broader responsibilities.

You will also need to consider whether you realistically have the manpower and expertise to take on this new task. While at first you may believe you have absolutely no more bandwidth, really outline what level of commitment will be required, how often, at what level, and who will perform the task. You will probably find that the task can be done, at least initially, with the resources you have. The most typical situation will be where you may have the manpower to complete a task or project in the short term; however, a long term commitment will require additional resources. Take on a responsibility for a short period of time and show that you are the right person for the job and that the task is important to the company before asking for additional support. Asking for resource up front has a few negative impacts:

- If you aren't able to gain approval quickly or at all, it puts completion of the task at risk
- If you are able to proceed with the task after additional resource requests are denied, management will perceive that you irresponsibly requested unnecessary resources
- Expectations are far higher when additional expense has been committed to the responsibility

If after much consideration you decide that additional resources and or expertise are necessary to take on this responsibility, even in the short run, then you will need to put together a summary that outlines a description of the responsibility, the frequency of completing the associated tasks, the potential benefits to groups throughout the company, the timing of completing the initial task, what resources and associated costs are required, why they are necessary, and how you determined or calculated what level of additional resource are needed. Be prepared to present this opportunity to your manager or, if appropriate, your peers to gain additional support in preparation for the proposal to management.

Before beginning, you must ask yourself if this task is already being performed somewhere else within the company. If your desire to take on this responsibility is due to poor or incomplete execution by another team, stop the idea of owning the responsibility right now. I've seen very few cases where taking on another group's responsibilities hasn't been perceived as a negative way to approach the issue. No one likes to be told they are incompetent or unable to perform a task, even if it is true.

In the event you feel a responsibility should be migrated from one group to another, it should be migrated as a result of an operational reorganization or some other tactful method. For example, if the IT department holds responsibility for running certain technical processes, but you feel they'd be better run in your organization since your group is responsible for correcting errors in the process, you may have a valid argument. This would be an example where the line of responsibility is gray and the process in total might be more efficient if it were reorganized. Another example would be a case where the Marketing department reports sales numbers because they once had responsibility for the sales reporting tool. However, for the last three years the sales organization has been responsible for the sales tool. Perhaps, then, sales reporting should move from Marketing to the Sales team due to the migration of expertise from one group to another over time. Whatever the rationale for moving an existing responsibility into your organization, it will be most successful if the group relinquishing the process as well as the other effected organizations understand and agree with the rationale.

Once you've identified this new responsibility, how do you actually take on the new role?

Let's assume that you have identified the perfect responsibility to bring into your group. No other organization is currently performing the process, you believe it would be helpful to other organizations, and you could at least initially build and run the process with no additional resources. Let's use Amy's example of customer profit margin reporting from the "Be Strategic" tip.

First things first. If you have employees, walk them through the initial design of the process. Ensure that your employees understand the benefits to the organization, what role they might play in the process, and make sure to solicit any potential risks of successful completion from your staff. There may be constraints you haven't considered or perhaps you've relied on time or expertise that may not truly be available once you've fleshed out the process with your team. If that is the case, your team will appreciate the opportunity to help in resolution of the constraints. Remember, everyone wants to be part of a success. Your employees will likely feel the same way once they understand that this is an opportunity for them to gain positive exposure and earn respect from other organizations. If you have no direct employees, then just be certain that you've considered all of the possible constraints before committing yourself to the responsibility.

Once you have support from your team, it is time to approach your manager. It is important that your manager be aware and supportive of the tasks you are about to bring into the organization. Remember, your success (and sometimes your failure) reflect upon your manager as well. Additionally, there is nothing more embarrassing than your peers or boss becoming aware of a new process in your group before you have discussed it with your manager. Requesting a formal meeting with your supervisor to discuss your ideas is a good place to start. You should come prepared with a short presentation or a summary of talking points and numerical data, if appropriate. Try not to take more than thirty minutes, certainly not more than an hour. If your manager is exceptionally interested, she will find additional time to continue the discussion.

Once your supervisor has blessed the process, it's time to rally your troops and begin cursory communication with the organizations that may be affected, may benefit from, and may be providing information to support your new responsibility. Whether you meet with each of these organizations separately or as a team is up to you. That decision should be driven by the culture of the company and the type of responsibility. When discussing the process with those groups impacted, remember they may be resistant to change, may feel the process will impede their workflow, and may be generally unappreciative of the effort. It's your objective to gain their support. Though this isn't always possible, be sure to highlight the benefits to the rest of the organization and find a way for them to be part of the success, either through team involvement or input into the way in which the process is designed.

The new responsibilities will likely be well received by those groups who benefit from the change. Ensure during these discussions that you gain insight into any concerns they may have about the quality of the final product. These discussions will assist you in understanding any process shortfalls and will expand the company's support for your new responsibilities.

There is one last word of advice concerning this tip: Be careful not to overuse or abuse this approach. No one likes a do-gooder or a know-it-all, no matter how much good they may be doing or how much they know. You should always be open to new opportunities to expand your role or expertise, but be cognizant that others may perceive this as encroaching on their territory or in some other way as being overzealous. Be sensitive to the response of other teams and individuals who could create challenges to a successful process or who could strain your reputation. It is often effective to include them in the process or, if need be, augment your initial approach to reduce any anxiety in others.

Lastly, pick your battles. Do not offer to take on responsibility simply for the sake of being a Superwoman. You should be confident that your approach is executable and that it will add real value to the company.

If you aren't certain you have all the information you need to assess whether you are ready to take this approach, become more deeply educated with the help of the next tip.

Tip 14: Get Your Hands Dirty

No, we're not referring to the need to hone your gardening skills or reinvigorate your childlike enthusiasm for mud-pie making. Sometimes you need to get into the lowest bowels of your role in the company and deal with the minutia. The best way to become the subject matter expert in an area is to build the processes yourself from the ground up, or dissect it yourself from the top down.

You may have taken many jobs in your career where during the first month you realized you were in over your head. It may not have been that you were lacking the technical or managerial skills for the job, but the new area may have been such a huge disaster it almost seemed irreparable. You *can* be successful in this instance but it requires you to rethink and redevelop the existing processes in the organization. This can't be done effectively unless you are able to sit in the seat of each person on your team or sit behind the wheels of each existing process and either run or fully describe it yourself. This is getting your hands dirty, touching all of the data yourself and seeing each process run with your own eyes and at the lowest levels. Your first instinct will be to rely on the opinion of others or to trust that your employees are doing everything in the best way possible and that they will be able to communicate the real issues to you. But remember, you were hired to run this area and solve the problems at hand and you need to understand how these areas work. Assess the processes not only as a manager or bystander but as a participant.

Don't be concerned that your questioning and involvement will make your employees believe you don't trust them or that they aren't doing a good job. Remember, everyone wants to be part of a success and employees want bosses who truly understand their issues and who are there to support them. If you approach your employees as a partner in understanding the challenges behind a process, they will be grateful for the attention as well as the opportunity to participate in change. You should never approach your employees or coworkers with an attitude which implies the current processes don't work, but with a helpful attitude indicating that you want to learn.

I was the Director of Revenue in a company in which the company's financial situation was very poor and the costs related to providing service to customers was in complete disarray. It was clear that the most immediate way to help the company was to reduce the company's monthly costs. So the CFO at the time asked me to take over the cost accounting department. Now, I've seen a number of messes in my career, but this mess by far topped the charts. The company was spending more than $50 million per month on direct customer costs and processing more than 20 thousand vendor invoices per month associated with these charges. The company really had very little idea whether or not the charges were appropriate or whether they were even needed to service the customers. There were three accountants managing the accounting and analysis for this area, and one had been laid off the week before I took over. Needless to say, we had our work cut out for us. It took about six months, but we completely overhauled every single process in this area and began providing data never before available and helped the company reduce its annual costs by millions of dollars. Without going into all the gory details, here is the approach we took, which can be used in many similar situations.

(In this scenario I was managing employees. However, if you aren't managing employees as part of the process, the same steps apply, only you may have to look to yourself as the sole source for the various skill-sets which may be necessary to improve a process. These are general steps, which you may have to bend somewhat to meet the needs of your process.)

1. To know where you want to go, you must first assess where you are today. So take inventory of the output for the processes you are managing as well as an inventory of which employees, if appropriate, are in charge of the outputs. For example: what types of reports are generated, how often, how are they distributed, what types of data are available from the output processes today, and does the data seem useful.

2. The next step is more difficult. Ask yourself what would be a useful output from the processes? You should set up a discussion with other organizations or your boss to assess what types of data would be useful, for what purposes might the data be utilized, what would be the optimal timing for distribution of the data, and what would be the "dream" reporting, task measurements, or information to produce. You may not be able to produce the "dream" process but knowing what people really want, how they plan on using that information, and what outcome your manager may be looking for will allow you to find the optimal output based on whatever information you are able to gather.

3. Based on your initial reviews and preliminary guidance, you will need to develop some objectives for the processes. These objectives could be anything from processing so many orders per hour, to completing certain tasks by a certain day of the month, to developing reporting and analysis to support other groups within the organization.

4. Now it's time to rally the troops (i.e. other coworkers impacted, or yourself if you're not managing a staff). You need to communicate the new or revised objectives with your group. You must gain their support prior to changing their processes and their trust that the changes will benefit

the company. Remember, everyone wants to be part of something successful and this is their opportunity to shine.

5. Now, start the rebuilding or revision initiative. Remember, you complete a grand task by taking one step at a time. At first the changes may seem overwhelming. Don't allow yourself to be paralyzed by the prospect of large changes. Likewise, don't allow yourself to shortcut improvements because you believe they are taking too long to complete. Break the project down into more measurable tasks and develop due dates for when you believe each task can be completed. From there you will use the skills you probably learned in school or in previous projects in order to complete the various tasks by their deadlines.

6. Once you're ready to unveil the changes, communicate the changes in process, output, or reporting to anyone who might be affected and don't forget to get their feedback on the final product. A word of caution: People will tell you what doesn't work properly or will complain about what information is still not available. Do not let their critique of the process bring you down. Use the feedback to make future improvements and be gracious for the feedback. Change is difficult and if another party was not initially involved, they might feel the final feedback is their opportunity to be part of the process.

A final word on process change: your hard work may not always end in success. Remember; despite all your efforts, you will still make a few mistakes. And if you don't make a few mistakes, you probably haven't made enough decisions. But if after all your hard work and changes the impact is still not what you were looking for—or worse, the outcome is less favorable than where you started—this next tip is for you.

Tip 15: Don't Let Your Mistakes Define Your Work

Today I had one of the lower days in my career. If you have been gifted with all pleasant work days then you are fortunate. But at some point in your career you will say "Wow, this was a really terrible day and I feel like a complete failure." After you finish thrashing yourself for your imperfections and scolding yourself for shortcomings, remember that no one is perfect and neither are you.

I am currently the Chief Financial Officer for a company and we are having some incredibly difficult financial times. Consequently, we are meeting with various potential new investors and lenders to obtain additional financial support for the business. Well I've had no less than ten face-to-face meetings, a dozen or so conference calls, and countless hours behind the computer developing the analysis necessary for this process over the past few weeks. Needless to say I am tired, overworked, impatient, and just a wee bit snappy. In a meeting with one of the more likely investors last week I made countless errors in judgment regarding what to say, when to speak up, and what not to say. Of course I've been somewhat depressed all week about the event, but didn't hit the low point until my boss, the Chief Executive Officer, called me into his office this morning and explained to me how poorly he felt the meeting had gone. I think his words were something like "the absolute worst meeting we've had" followed by a long list of my failures during the event.

So what is there to take from this life lesson? I mustered up the courage to sit down and type this tip after a long, depressing day at the office and a few glasses of wine. You will make mistakes, but you will prevail and all of your hard work will pay off, in this life or the next. Again, you and I will make mistakes. If you don't make a few then you are not giving it enough effort. There is a fine line between success and failure, and you will be successful in your career so long as you step to the right side of that line more often than not. Good luck in your efforts and don't let the mistakes today overshadow your efforts tomorrow. Learn from them, take notes, or simply file them away until you are ready to look at them in the light of a better day.

So what came of this really terrible day (which, ironically, was Good Friday)? Well, I had all weekend to feel sorry for myself as well as prepare for Monday's events. The next meeting went OK, not great, but satisfactorily. My boss thanked me for the hard work, though I don't think he was overly impressed. While I didn't make any glaring errors in judgment today, the so-so outcome did remind me that when you err on the side of not giving it your all, you'll produce mediocre results. I know you are tired of me saying "don't be afraid to make a mistake" and "push the envelope". And I know you're thinking, are you crazy, that's also how you get fired. Well, for those of you who need a rule of thumb regarding mediocrity and those average or less-than-average days, this next tip is for you.

Tip 16: Follow the Rule of Threes

Now surely you've heard the old adage that bad things come in threes. Maybe you've been lucky at the craps table with the number three or maybe you feel more like one of the three blind mice, but whatever your perspective, there is a rule of thumb to most things. In business success, too, you can follow the rule of threes.

This means that you should be willing to put yourself out there three times before pulling back into your shell. The odds are that you will fail probably once; that's less than half the time, so that's not so intimidating, right? It is unlikely you'll kill your career or internal drive with two lackluster or failed attempts, thus three attempts is perfect. So in your current position, the next time you want to take a stand on a new idea, process, or strategy, don't be afraid. Do your homework, follow a few of the steps and tips we've already discussed, and go for it. If at first you don't succeed try on the next and then the next opportunity you come across. You will be surprised at how much you learn from your first attempt at something big and different. The second and maybe third try will present you with even wiser ideas.

Now the rule of threes also works in your career choice, so don't be afraid to jump off the career cliff a few times, or even more if you're the daring type.

Earlier in my career I was an associate at a large foreign bank. At that time the bank was the largest bank in the world (this was before the US bank mergers in the late 90s). I had just been promoted, and believed I had a bright future with the bank. However, the foreign markets were in turmoil, so our bank was unable to participate in a large number of transactions in the US due to a weak foreign currency. Because of the times, I spent more energy on my wardrobe than doing new deals, and I was getting a little bored. So, when my husband introduced me to the CEO of this itsy bitsy company where he worked, I was more than willing to help out. What fun, helping a startup company build its financial models.

So I decided to leave the largest bank in the world to work for one of the smallest companies on Earth. I think we had monthly revenue of $100 when I started (and no I am not exaggerating, I really mean one hundred dollars). But it was great fun and it was an Internet company. We were the first company in the country to be "100% 56K modems," which tells you about when this happened. But the word "Internet" was on everyone's lips, and while no one knew what we would do with the Internet yet, I knew I would be a millionaire by the time it was all over. Except that I left before the company was sold for very little, and I never made any money. But, if I hadn't leaped, I would have always regretted it.

So, where am I now on the spectrum of career leaps? I'm currently considering a second potential leap as I type this tip. I don't want to jinx it, so maybe we'll save it for the sequel. For the next tip, it is a good time to talk about looking back at your life in order to brighten your future.

Tip 17: No Regrets

Don't walk through your life with great regrets. Everyone says that, and I really mean it. Your personal life is just as important as your career regarding regret, and regret is a damaging emotion. On a personal note, I do have one major regret in my career, which can't be rectified at this point, and one personal regret, which was rectified last year. I feel so strongly about this topic that I suggest, first, that you put this book down right now and go take care of any great regrets in your life which can still be rectified. Then hurry back.

Regarding my career regret, I was a relatively young analyst during the boom of the late 1990s. I had stock options in my company which were worth about $1,000,000 and were fully vested at the time. Now I am older and wiser and have rules surrounding personal wealth. I have a rule that if you ever have stock, savings, or anything else in one investment that exceeds a year's salary at your current job, you should sell or diversify those interests if at all possible. Could you imagine working for someone for a year for free? Well that's how I came to this very sophisticated rule for investment strategy. Who could bear losing a year's salary in one market crash? But that's exactly what happened in 2000. I lost $1,000,000 in the market because I didn't exercise my options when able. I stupidly thought the company was going to the moon. I have a friend who says you can never lose money by taking it off the table. She is so very right. Thus, when making a decision to do or not do something in your career, consider what the stark alternative to that decision might be. If the stark alternative is not palatable then you may be making the wrong decision.

Now, regarding those regrets in your career or personal life that can still be rectified, for goodness sakes what are you waiting for? A year ago on my birthday, I turned to my husband and said you know, I don't have a lot of great regrets in life (he was there for the year 2000 stock option debacle, so he quickly reminded me of that event). However, I then realized that I regretted not acting since college. I was very involved in theatre in high school and somewhat in college. But afterwards, I became so busy in my career and with life that I stopped auditioning and quit thinking about acting all together. My husband is super supportive, so he told me to get back out there and break a leg. And I did! I was cast in four feature films last year. Of course, they may never see the light of day, but I have an acting resume now, and an agent to boot. No regrets...Not anymore...

You can do it too—just get out there and break a leg (unless your great regret is that you've never run a marathon. Then by all means be careful not to break a leg out there, but get out there). And getting back to your career, if you've finally made the decision to leave your company in an attempt to have no further regrets, then this next tip is for you.

Tip 18: Know Thyself (Or at Least Thy Worth)

To say you must "know thyself" means you must be honest with yourself regarding not only how well or poorly you negotiate but at what point you are willing to walk away from a new opportunity. This is the only tip where I conducted some level of market research. I'll share the very interesting results of those findings regarding women and salary negotiation shortly. However, let's first talk turkey. The truth is you have a minimum number you'd be willing to accept whether that is through base pay, bonus, or benefits to take a new position or to stay in your current one. You surely have a desired number in your head. We all know you aim higher, hope for somewhere near your target, and absolutely freak out if they come in below what you can live with. Now, many women are bulldogs when it comes to haggling on behalf of their companies but are terrible at fighting for their own compensation. Why is this?

I have almost as much experience as a hiring manager as being on the other side of the table and I'll tell you flat out: women do not negotiate. And when they do it is almost never as successful as the male counterpart interviewing in the room next to them. From the hiring side, when women begin to negotiate their compensation they invariably provide some basis or rationale for the higher compensation. The basis is typically personal, something like "My kid starts college next year," or "We just bought a house," or "I have these huge student loans," etc. Men, on the other hand, never give a reason; they simply say "This is what I'm worth." And you know what? That's all that matters. There is no point in bringing emotion or personal life into it. You are worth the compensation and that's what you should be paid. I had a conversation with a very good friend of mine about six months ago regarding this very issue. She is a very accomplished partner at a prestigious law firm in New York and has no reason to believe she isn't worth every penny she makes. However, she was coming up for her partner review and was discussing strategy regarding the coming year's compensation negotiation with me in preparation. Mind you, she is a very smart attorney, but the first thing she did when discussing her strategy was to bring up her personal financial needs. You see, even smart attorneys fall victim to this problem. Also remember when you do tell them what you want and they sit there in silence, you should stay silent as well. Do not start rambling on about your personal financial situation or backing down.

We've all read the studies and surveys that claim that women make less than men for the same job. If you are doubtful, please spend some time doing your own research on the topic. It's absolutely true. One of my more favorite and seemingly more progressive supervisors actually disagreed with me on this point. He said he didn't believe that women made less than men when in the same or similar job. My response was to remind him that while I was the Chief Financial Officer of the company, arguably one of the highest ranking jobs in the company, the company had hired a male Vice President of Operations a month after me and given him a higher salary. Now, here comes the important part of this story: my supervisor wasn't even aware of that fact, though he had approved the hiring for both of us within the same 30 day period. The point in mentioning this is that women do not make less than men because men are evil and manipulative, but that women make less than men because women do not negotiate well enough. And if you think you *do* negotiate then this next section is for you (and remember, "know thyself").

In developing this tip a survey across 100 people was conducted in an attempt to assess to what extent women negotiated more poorly than men and perhaps discover the root to this phenomenon. This was not a highly scientific research study; however, the results did provide some insight and perhaps will round out this tip. Before we get into the results, let's discuss the population surveyed and the questions they were asked.

I sent a request to a number of people in the business world with an anonymous survey and asked them to in turn send it to others they knew in business. It was sent largely to executives and people who had reached some level of success in their career. The first 100 surveys returned were accepted and the data set simply ended there. The final data set had the following demographics:

	Women	Men	Total
Respondents	51	49	100
Average Years in the Workforce	20.0	20.6	20.3

At first glance this looks like a pretty level data set. 65% of the men answered that they were either in upper or executive management or were professionals or entrepreneurs. This compares to only 57% of the women. So that points to two considerations: one, that men are more likely to move into more successful roles with relatively similar years of work experience; and two, that base-dollar compensation wouldn't be a useful comparison. So, in the trek to identify relative negotiation skills between men and women, the survey looked to percentage improvements in salary versus absolute changes.

The respondents were also asked "What's the highest % increase in compensation you have been able to negotiate above what was initially offered by a potential employer?" Before you learn what they said, let's first look at how well both men and women felt about their negotiation skills.

The respondents were asked "How often do you negotiate higher compensation than initially offered by an employer?" Of the female respondents, 43% replied that they either usually or always negotiate their salary. This compared to 58% of the men that usually or always negotiated their salary. So part one of this tip is for goodness' sakes, women, negotiate! Do not take the salary they offer you right off the bat. If they tell you in the offer conversation that there is no room to negotiate, do *not* believe them. If you counter with a higher compensation, the worst they will do is say they can't meet your request. It will then be up to you to decide what you're willing to live with. If they were interested enough in your skill-set to offer you a position, they are not going to pull the offer away simply because you requested a higher compensation. They are expecting you to push back to some extent, even if they have little or no room to move.

So if you are part of the 43% that do negotiate your salary, then you can pat yourself on the back, but don't get too comfortable. How do you know you negotiated a good deal? In the survey when women were asked the question "What's the highest % increase in compensation you have been able to negotiate above what was initially offered by a potential employer?" the average increase across those who responded was 10%. When men were asked the same question, the answer was 15%. So is 5% a huge difference? Yes it is; The Institute for Women's Policy Research reported that the ratio of women's to men's median annual earnings was 77% for full-time, year-round workers in 2009. [1] I'm sure you're thinking, well the difference in the survey was only 5%, not 23%, so what gives? Well, remember, if every time you change jobs you receive a 10% increase in income versus 15%? Then after twenty years in the work force you will make substantially less than your male counterpart. The US Department of Labor reported that the average employee holds a position for between three and five years, with the shorter duration between the ages of 18 and 38. [2] So if I take two typical college graduates with the same starting income, one female, one male, and look at what the impact of the variance in salary negotiation means over the 20 years of

---

[1] http://www.iwpr.org/pdf/C350.pdf

[2] America's Dynamic Workforce: 2006; U.S. Department of Labor

professional work experience following graduation, we could calculate the following:

Assumptions:
Both employees change jobs every four years
Both employees start with a base salary of $30,000 out of college
Female receives a 10% increase each job change
Male receives a 15% increase each job change

Age	Male Salary	Female Salary	Years in Workforce	Female Salary % Male Salary
21	$30,000	$30,000	0	100%
25	$34,500	$33,000	4	96%
29	$39,675	$36,300	8	91%
33	$45,626	$39,930	12	88%
37	$52,470	$43,923	16	84%
41	$60,341	$48,315	20	80%
45	$69,392	$53,147	24	77%
49	$79,801	$58,462	28	73%

As you can see it's not hard to see why the US Department of Labor reports that women make only 77% of their male counterparts. It is very likely that of the 100 people in this sample, the same average phenomenon exists as well.

Now if you are like a few of the women that first heard this theory, you may be saying "I always negotiate and I think I negotiate pretty well." No one can confirm whether or not you have well-honed negotiation skills; however as part of the survey I asked a few questions surrounding the respondents' youth to try to identify some correlation between youthful habits and negotiation skills. This section was somewhat surprising. I assumed (for whatever unscientific reason) going into the survey that a higher level of aggression and direct negotiation experience as a child would influence skills as an adult. The following questions were asked, with this assumption in mind:

- Did you engage in trades of property as a youth (i.e. baseball cards, my bike for your skateboard, etc.)
- Were your parents willing to let you explain your side of an issue or negotiate as a child
- Have you ever been in a fight or forced to physical confrontation
- What were your favorite sports, games, and hobbies as a kid

I evaluated each respondent's answer to these questions in conjunction with their response from the survey question "What's the highest % increase in compensation you have been able to negotiate above what was initially offered by a potential employer?" In all the responses to each of the questions, there was absolutely no mathematical correlation in any way between the answers to these questions and how well the respondent negotiated. It was very confusing. It seemed there just *had* to be some insight to gleam from all of this information that might help a woman assess whether she was likely to negotiate a stronger salary based on her experiences. This could be an important bit of information. Because no matter how well you believe you negotiate in compensation discussions, if you are aware that you may be predisposed to less successful negotiations, you can then adjust your approach.

So while there weren't any mathematical correlations, there were some consistent patterns between the sports and hobbies the respondents played as children and how well they negotiated as adults. It didn't seem to matter if the respondents were male or female or if they participated in certain sports or hobbies as children; they had either a consistently stronger or weaker experience when negotiating as an adult.

As a child if you played chess, card games, or were a dancer, you were likely a stronger negotiator than your counterpart, regardless of your sex. The first two made sense; however, dance was seemingly unusual. I still haven't quite broken the code on why someone who participated in dance as a youth would be a stronger negotiator as an adult, however a few people have put forward the hypothesis that because dance requires one to understand the rules and moves of the game or your partner, that this skill would make one better at reading other parties and pushing boundaries during a negotiation. Makes some sense, I suppose. While no physical sport stood out as an indicator of strong negotiation skills, two sports were more typical activities of stronger negotiators: tennis and swimming. While I have no scientific answer to the reason why these two sports would rise to the top; after discussion with those who were involved in these sports as a youth, we came to a few conclusions. Both sports are based on very controlled form and finesse. In order to excel at either of these sports you must focus and spend time making small adjustments in your form to achieve great results. The same could be said for strong negotiation skills.

And another weird finding: If you were really into arts & crafts, drawing, reading, fishing, music, or instruments, you are likely a poorer negotiator than your counterpart. Of course, I did all of those things, which may explain why even now I make less than I should in my current job. Those respondents who golfed, biked, and skied tended to have weaker negotiating skills.

Despite a whirlwind of findings, the tip remains to always target at least a 15% increase above your initial or base offer in your next role, do not settle for less (and if you participate in any activities which might indicate weaker negotiation skills, push much harder than you think you really should to get your increase and change your hobbies immediately). Don't cut yourself short, remember you are worth it and you don't have to defend your request with personal reasons. Now once you feel you've evolved, you're earning a reasonable wage, and you are moving into the high point of your career, heed this next bit of advice.

Tip 19: Find Your Poise

Not many women routinely find a level of poise that takes them to the next level in their career. My husband told me a few days ago that nothing unnerves a man like a woman who can present with no emotion, completely rationally, and be silent long enough for the other people in the room to become uncomfortable. He said men have a hard time understanding women anyway, and when you add the ability to out-poise the men in the room, men are completely at a loss. And you know what, he is right. This tip is thus dedicated to my husband, who helps me find my poise.

So what *is* poise? Well, I have a high school friend in town this weekend and she has a great level of experience in dealing with very tenuous situations and relationships in her job, so she was extremely helpful in distilling the definition for me as we floated down the river in a few inner tubes on a hot Texas day. We decided that poise is different for everyone, but at its base it is the ability to focus on the task at hand and pull out the calm-and-collected communication style that is needed to successfully complete the task. Poise may be your ability to be patient in a situation, or calculating, or logical, or well spoken, or social, or funny, or maybe it is just the ability to be quiet and listen. I'm sure you've seen poise in action. A few of our presidents have had it, that ability to calmly explain a position and regardless of your political stance, you think "That was a pretty good answer." Maybe it is the way one of your mentors always says the right thing at the right time. If you think of a person you have worked with and admire greatly, you will see that they have some level of poise in the way they approach their work. Perhaps you can't put your finger on it, but you know it's impressive.

So we all want it, that poise, that "je ne sais quoi," but how do you get it? I personally struggle with this question and honestly, it is one of the last frontiers for my personal development. If you have poise you'll likely do well in business, but unfortunately, it's hard to teach. You have to be faced with a situation where you can practice it. And as I found out this week at work, the more rehearsed and prepared for the event, the more likely your poise is to come out and shine.

During this last week I have had to provide analysis for some executives of my company to be used as the basis for negotiations with one of our investors. Now, the outcome of these negotiations has no impact on me personally, but it is my job to support management, our investors, and our Board of Directors during the process. So what happens when you are in the middle of all of these parties and they are negotiating? Well you start hearing the term "fall guy" and "patsy" in the back of your head. If something gets ugly, I could be one of those terrible scapegoats, and that is simply not a good career move. So as the process went last week, I sent out the requested analysis and I received an email from one of the parties with a laundry list of complaints about the analysis, both logical and emotional but all ending with "You know this type of work has consequences..." Well honestly, that sounded a little bit like a threat to my job and my livelihood, so needless to say I was an incredible wreck that night. All parties were scheduled to discuss the analysis as well as the rationale behind the assumptions the next morning.

Fortunately, my high school friend and husband, who have both already found their poise, coached me that evening. What did the preparation look like? Well, here's what we did:

- Walked through each of the arguments against my work and assumptions
- Dissected the potential reasons for each of the arguments, both obvious and less obvious

- Succinctly developed the support for each point or assumption in my analysis
- Identified a way to show that each point I had made was in line with or at least not inconsistent with comments the disagreeing party had made in previous discussions
- Wrote an outline for my points and arguments
- Role-played and practiced the order of my points, and the way in which I would present them

After going through this process, the key critiques received from my husband and friend were:

- "Be more succinct." I have a habit of repeating myself when I'm trying to make a point. Repeating yourself and describing your position in multiple ways only lessens the strength of your argument. Say it once and say it succinctly.
- "Remain calm and show no emotion; keep to the side of logic." I am passionate about everything in life, so it is difficult to maintain a calm and level voice and diction when I feel strongly about a position. But remember, emotion is often perceived as weakness and it is imperative in business that you show limited emotion even when faced with an emotional discussion.
- "Use silence." Let me repeat myself, silence.......An uncomfortable silence is worth its weight in gold during any discussion. If you are comfortable with your answer to a question or you feel complete in your statement, remain silent. Let the other party take the next word. Don't fill empty air with your blather, let the silence ride.

So the next morning I had the dreaded conference call with all parties and the first half of the call was largely dedicated to my analysis and the disagreeing party's attempts to dismantle it. I went through the points and stuck to my outline. When I was asked something unexpected, I counted to five before providing an answer. My answers were calm save for a few times where I went a little off the rails, but all in all, I was succinct. I was mindful not to repeat myself and was silent after each time I delivered an answer to a question. There was once such a long pause after my response to a question that one party actually asked "Are you guys still there?" Of course at that point I muted myself and gave myself a little high five and a giggle. So was the call a success? Well, I wish the call hadn't been necessary at all, but I gained a great deal of poise practice and I think all parties were impressed with my ability to perform under pressure.

So find your own poise. At some point in your career you will become aware of the shortcomings in your personal communication style. My preparation in the scenario above may be completely different than your preparation. Maybe you are seen as too uptight and as a stick in the mud. Maybe in that situation preparation is less of the path to finding your poise, and maybe about finding a way to loosen up during a contentious meeting. Whatever the weaknesses in your communication style, you have to develop a way to temper them and find your poise.

The best way is to ask for advice, like I did. Don't be afraid to engage others that you trust to provide helpful critique. When you are young and ambitious, you often think the best way to move forward in your career is to push harder and make decisions on your own. You assumed because you were closer to the situation that no one else would really be able to provide the right advice. Surely, without the entire context of the situation and the players, another person couldn't *possibly* have the knowledge necessary to help. Now, if this is how you often feel when someone tries to give you advice in business, this next and last tip is absolutely for you.

Tip 20: Learn to Take a Tip

This tip may sound the most ridiculous because the fact that you are reading this book indicates that you are open to tips on your career. However, it's important to discuss this point because many women are hesitant to listen to others when given advice. As I have matured (or aged, let's be frank) I have begun to provide guidance and tips to women working for me and to friends *when asked*. Don't, however, give unsolicited advice to women; because they don't usually want it, I included, at least when I was younger. I'll take all the advice I can get now, though I still struggle sometimes with the fear of looking incompetent. There it is. Women so often don't want any advice or help because they don't want to look incompetent or as if they don't deserve the position they currently have. If you didn't learn from others' mistakes you'd have to make all of them on your own and that's crazy—believe me, you will make plenty of mistakes, even with good advice. If you take the advice of others maybe you'll make fewer, though, and your career will benefit.

For this tip I thought it was important that I took my own advice and asked others for a tip to give to women who were looking to advance their careers in corporate America. These tips are from people well admired and from people who are admired by others. Both men and women contributed to these suggestions. And while they were told they could remain anonymous, some agreed to be quoted, so here are some tips from successful professionals across the country. Maybe a few will provide additional guidance you have been looking for throughout this somewhat long-winded book.

1. Find a solid avenue for building and maintaining your self-confidence and self-esteem: women's business

groups, professional development online blogs, industry mentoring resources, etc. Private business is a challenge and your mental approach to it is crucial.

2. Keep your priorities straight.

3. Vendors can often provide intelligence about job openings at their clients' companies. Make outreach to former vendors part of your job search strategy.

4. Don't be afraid to listen to your gut and do what feels right to you, even if it isn't what others are telling you that you "should" do.

5. Speak your mind, pleasantly.

6. Always be willing to learn from other colleagues and mentors—male and female alike.

7. Do bring your unique personality to your management style; just be aware that there are rules, mainly unwritten ones set by males. Take time to understand the rules of your particular game.

8. Create your list of mentors early in your career.

9. Use your voice and do not automatically defer to those in higher positions; some of the very best ideas received are from the ranks and by speaking up you will gain respect if well executed.

10. You need to be your own advocate.

11. Don't be afraid to speak up in meetings. Don't be afraid to ask the hard questions.

12. Always think before you speak! Behave as you think the "perfect" boss, supervisor, etc. should, even if you don't always feel like it.

13. Research salaries for similar positions in the area, objectively look at what you have to offer the employer

that will help their bottom line, think about what you want to say and don't take anything personally. Ask and don't go on and on. Don't be the first to say a dollar amount and be comfortable with silence—the first one who talks after you ask usually loses.

14. State university works fine for undergrad degree. Spend the dollars for a better name on a graduate degree. Go for the best title and best salary upfront. Once inside, increases and promotions are mostly incremental.

15. I think the key to being successful as a female professional and executive is not to focus on the fact that you're female. Be great at your profession, go above and beyond, create value every day, bring solutions not problems, be a lifelong learner, remember that your employees are people, create balance in your life, and believe that you can achieve everything you want to achieve.

16. Try something different in the workplace. Organizations want women to be involved in nontraditional areas. We have the opportunity to be and do things differently than they have always been done. Knowing who you are can lead this journey in the workplace to great places. We must keep doing it!

17. Take continuing education/college courses relevant to work to keep your edge; always look for ways to improve the work flow. Be creative and a good listener, everyone's ideas are important to achieving success.

18. Don't be afraid to ask for more than you expect to get. It allows room to negotiate. Dress well, even in a casual environment. Others will think more highly of you.

19. Be willing to walk away. Negotiate like you do not need the job.

20. Listen to your instincts. Find a job where you can utilize your strengths and are allowed to be candid. Don't settle! Find a mentor and be a mentor. Share your knowledge

with others and learn from them. Ask for help when you need it.

—Julie Kirk, Sr. Vice President

21. Confidence is the key. Know what your strengths are and play upon these to the fullest. Take the emphasis off what you don't do well (we tend to do this) and redirect this energy on what you do well.

—Laurie Canepa, Partner/ Director

22. We make choices every day. Make sure that for every choice you make, you own and are accountable for that choice.

23. People work for passionate people, passionately! (I just made this up by the way, I think...) I believe the three most important trends in successful managers: like the job, love the company, adore the staff.

—My little sister, Frankie Guynes

24. Always remember business is business. Work hard and do not take it personally if things don't always go your way. If you are passionate, believe in yourself and treat others with respect, your efforts will be recognized and success will come your way (eventually—be patient).

25. I became more successful and satisfied in my professional endeavors when I got over a feeling of entitlement, accepted that respect was about what I owe others, and when I established a network of folks outside of my immediate workgroup whom I trusted to give honest constructive advice that I allowed to transform me.

—Sandra Hale-DeMarco, Business
Analyst Global Finance Operations

26. Be adaptable and creative. There are many approaches to solve problems other than the traditional approach.

27. Please ASK! Ask for a raise, promotion, better office, perks—even if you are thinking that it doesn't define you - it defines you to other people.

—Melynda Caudle, President

28. Try to separate the typical female tendencies of being the "pleaser" and view your business relationships completely differently from your personal relationships.

29. Learn to say no.

30. Find your inspiring goals both professionally and personally that keep you excited to get out of bed each morning and pursue them with everything you have!
    —Lori Arnold, President

31. My advice is for new mothers or soon to be mothers in the business world. Before you have children, it's easy to think that you'll go back to work and be the professional working mom. Keep in mind though that you cannot get the time back that you missed with your children as babies and toddlers, but you can always pick your career back up where you left off. You'll never regret the decision to put your career on hold to enjoy that precious time with your children.

32. Be reliable and trustworthy.

33. Always give 100% and negotiate your pay upward; never lower you standard to meet your pay.
    —My mother, Debbie Lewis

34. Mentally be like Katherine Hepburn or Lucille Ball...don't accept or tolerate glass ceilings or gender as an obstacle.

35. Find that match where your talent can best be utilized by a manager who needs that talent and will put up with the need for flexibility if required. It can then lead to quicker management exposure.

36. Just because you don't see woman doing what you want to do does not mean you can't do it. Never feel that you do not belong.

37. Be confident in who you are.

38. Be professional, but don't be afraid to be yourself. US corporate culture needs a lot of changes to bring recognition/reward for value creation away from the "in guys" network and back towards actual value creators, and women can help bring those changes about. Stand up for yourself, and be prepared to pay the price when you do it, and don't blame repercussions for your choices on sexism, race, or some other arbitrary/sensitive criteria unless you can prove it.

39. Pick your issues/moments to press an issue. Some things are more important than others.

40. First, I think they deserve much more credit than they receive. That being said, I would suggest one (woman or man, for that matter) remain humble and not be too interested in their own story. I've met many a successful woman that had to work hard to get where they are and then boast it to any and everyone that would listen. Seek first to understand, and then be understood. Wise advice no matter where you are...at the bottom or the top of the organization.

41. Focus on driving people to clear decisions and actions and do not hold back in taking the same approach.

42. Quit being mean toward other women in the business world!

43. Be yourself, never compromise and never let people treat you as less than equal. Move before giving in. If you can't be yourself and be recognized for that, change the situation.

44. As you transition from being an individual contributor to management, and particularly as you move up the management ladder, you will receive less overt positive reinforcement from your supervisor. It is important to remember that the higher the position, the higher the expectations are for the individual in that position. Things you may have done at a lower management level that

garnered recognition may now be expected. Create your own energy and sense of worth...

45. Be mindful of the context—in my experience women tend to talk through ideas, solutions, concepts whereas men expect things to be more linear and less open ended.

46. Be yourself, be strong, and stay cool. Don't let anyone intimidate you. Don't let emotion cloud professional judgment. Be honest and have courage. Treat everyone from the bottom up with respect and dignity.

47. I typically have had somewhere around 40-50% of my work team as women, throughout my experience as a marketing professional and leader. I have found women on my team to be incredibly passionate, organized and empathetic, but typically they find it more difficult to create conflict when necessary to resolve an issue. This can hold them back relative to most men I've had on my team.

48. Do not try and be a man; women have different but as many business qualities as men do, so there is no need to be the same.

49. Don't giggle after you say something important or strong; the statement loses its power.

50. Don't attack other women in business. Women are so competitive with one another, they shouldn't be.

So that is it: twenty tips for corporate chicks. While there is no way a small read can by itself make a big change in your career, hopefully a few of the tips have provided you with some wisdom. Each of these tips I had to learn the hard way. If every woman could take the advice of another person to improve their career just a little, we'd push the gender further into the higher ranks of corporate America. So happy ladder-climbing, ladies, may you break a glass ceiling or two, and remember it's not a rat race if you're as cool as a cat.